TIGER

TIGER

The Making of a Sports Car

Mike Taylor

GENTRY BOOKS
LONDON

To Janet and Clive Fleay
for giving up so much of their time

First published 1979

ISBN 0 85614 052 X

Published by Gentry Books Limited,
16 Regency Street, London SW1.
Distributed in the USA by

Filmset by Trader Web Offset Limited,
Heanor Gate Estate, Heanor, Derbyshire.
Printed and bound in Great Britain at
William Clowes & Sons Limited,
Beccles and London.

Contents

Foreword

When Michael Taylor contacted me and asked if he could come and talk about Tigers as he intended to write a book on them, I was most intrigued to see what his attitude towards the car would be. It has always seemed to me that the Tiger is a car to which people react in very different ways.

Some approach the car trying to see how clever they can be by finding deficiencies, many of which are quite obvious. Others take the more sensible approach of seeing if they enjoy the car and they find that they do and that the deficiencies which are present don't matter if they decide to use the car normally and not seek out troubles. Michael Taylor's book I think brings out both these aspects of the car very successfully.

The Tiger was a bold venture by Rootes, representing a very significant step up in performance compared with any other production car they had made. The development was completed and production started in a remarkably short time span largely due to the enthusiasm of those involved who got 'bitten by the Tiger bug'. During the development period it was difficult to know just what standards of ride, handling, braking, etc, should be set as the concept gave little scope for changes if the cost were to be kept down. I believe a good compromise was reached for the American market which is where the car was aimed and perhaps surprisingly this compromise well suited the UK market, providing in a small sports car relaxed performance, together with comfort and adequate handling. It was also surprising how well the Tiger was capable of being developed into an effective car for rallying and racing without excessive expense on exotic conversion kits, etc.

The initial concentration on the American market meant that the car was not available in the UK in any large numbers for very long before American safety and emission legislation came out which would have meant major costly changes, the UK sales alone not justifying continuation. Chrysler came on the scene and production ceased. It is a pity as I believe that had the Tiger continued in production, it would have filled a gap in the market for a number of years.

Michael Taylor must have had a frustrating and bewildering time researching the information for this book. A great deal had to come from memory, not all records being available, and different peoples' memories are often conflicting and poor, particularly on such a subject as the Tiger where there are so many aspects to deal with.

I believe this book, apart from providing a factual record of the Tiger story, proves a fascinating tale of the unique way in which the Tiger was evolved and makes very good reading. Regrettably one wonders if in these days of increasing legislation, any similar project could go ahead so quickly and successfully.

Peter Wilson
Coventry, 1978

Introduction

It all began one evening some three years ago when two friends and myself were discussing Sunbeam Tigers. We concluded that, with the exception of magazine road tests, very little had been written about the Tiger, and as enthusiasts we were eager to learn as much as possible about this exciting motorcar. There and then, I decided to make a start, unearthing whatever material and information was available. Luckily, right from the beginning, my research was helped enormously by the many people still at Chrysler who were willing not only to talk about the car but who also remained enthusiastic. Clearly, there was no time for delay if I was going to try to record the entire story before it was lost forever.

In compiling this book, I have attempted to bring to light much of the hidden fact surrounding the Tiger, and, in so doing, possibly dispel some of the false rumours which have spread over the years. It is sad that in the period since 1967, Chrysler UK's constant changes in fortune have rendered many relevant documents unavailable and despite my efforts to tell the complete story, there are, perhaps, some details still left buried.

I must apologise for the lack of 'official' photographs concerning the first prototype Tigers. It is possible that some photos were taken of these cars (although it was not Rootes' policy to encourage photography of prototype vehicles) and I can only conclude that any such material must have been lost in the course of time. I am therefore indebted to those who have been good enough to loan me their personal 'snaps' to illustrate this narrative.

Meanwhile, I am extremely grateful to all those who have helped me and can only marvel at their ability to recall events which took place some fourteen years ago. They are all busy people and they freely gave up their time to relive the Tiger programme, just for my benefit.

I offer this work as a tribute to a 'rare' sports car, and to those people who have given me their help, advice, and encouragement. The order in which they are listed is simply alphabetical:

Roy Axe, Keith Ballisat, Alec Caine, Marcus Chambers, Colin Cook, Andrew Cowan, John Drew, George Fallehy, Charles Fisher, Alan Fraser, Ian Garrad, Tony Good of Good Relations, Peter Harper, Alan Hartwell, Clive Harrington, Roger Harold who took his Tiger to Coventry, Kenneth Howes, Alan Jones, E. M. Lea-Major, Leo Lesperance, Bob May, Chris McGovern, Eric Neale, Des O'Dell, John Panks, John Pellowe and the members of the AC Owners Club, John Newton, John Rowe, Carroll Shelby, Maurice A. Smith, Rosemary Smith, Doane Spencer, Lew Spencer, Meryl Sundberg, Don Tarbun, John Tidy, Bernard Unett, Peter Ware, John Weston-Hays, Ted White, and Peter Wilson.

In addition to the individuals mentioned above, I wish to thank the following for their help and co-operation: British Museum Newspaper Library, Colindale; Charing Cross Library, Westminster; Mare Street Library, Hackney; *Birmingham Evening Post; Coventry Evening Telegraph;* and The Society of Motor Manufacturers and Traders.

Mike Taylor
Tunbridge Wells

An Old Name A New Car

'It's a car one parks with reluctance, such is the fun in driving it.' So said *Autocar* magazine's road test of the Sunbeam Tiger in April 1965. Today, Tigers belong to an ever increasing breed of car known as 'classic'; enthusiasts are often willing to pay more for a good second-hand example than the car's original retail price some twelve or more years ago.

Sometimes thought of as a hybrid because of its Anglo- American amalgamation, the Tiger was Rootes' first and only venture into the high-performance sports car market. The installation of an American engine into a British-built body has been the salvation of many a company wishing to use a powerful, compact engine yet not wanting to become involved with the immense cost of developing one themselves — Jensen and Bristol are two such examples.

A comprehensive study of the Tiger must inevitably start with an appreciation of its parentage, and the background which led to its inception. In 1935, the Rootes Group successfully fused the engineering expertise of Hillman and Humber with the ailing but nevertheless very marketable names of Sunbeam and Talbot, with their enviable history of motor racing.

The Rootes Group was a family concern. At its helm as chairman was William, later Lord (he was knighted First Baron Rootes of Ramsbury in 1959) 'Billy' Rootes, with his younger brother, Sir Reginald, as financial advisor. Lord Rootes' sons, Brian and Geoffrey, were in charge of sales and manufacture respectively, while Sir Reginald's son Timothy was responsible for servicing. Those who knew

Norman Garrad at the wheel of a Talbot Alpine. Based on a prototype built by George Hartwell, this car was produced between 1953 and 1955, taking its name from the Alpine Rally in which the Rootes rally team had been so successful. (Photo: Chrysler UK)

Lord Rootes found him to be forceful, forthright, and impulsive. Rootes' cars were solid and reliable, but lacked individuality, with no pretence to power or performance. Indeed, Lord Rootes seemed quite unmoved by sports cars or motor sport of any kind, and was content to let firms such as MG and Jaguar monopolize this area of the market.

But within the company was a man who would ultimately persuade Rootes to change his mind; that man was Norman Garrad. Garrad realized the benefits to be had from a successful competitions team and approached Lord Rootes with his proposals. Lord Rootes finally agreed, and Garrad set about establishing the Rootes competitions department in 1948. Before long, he had accumulated a formidable collection of drivers. At the time, the current production saloon was the Sunbeam Talbot. Unfortunately, with its 2.2 litre ohv engine the car was not entirely suitable for competition use, being somewhat heavy and underpowered.

Nevertheless, the team was very successful, and created a considerable amount of good publicity.

With an active competitions department established, Rootes were anxious to introduce a more sporting model into their range. Thus, when George Hartwell suggested producing a two-seater version of the Sunbeam Talbot, Lord Rootes readily agreed, deciding to call the car Sunbeam Alpine in honour of the Rootes Rally Team successes on the Alpine Rally. Introduced in 1953, it featured the same mechanics as the saloon, but utilized an open two-door bodyshell.

In the event, the 'Talbot' Alpine remained in production for a mere two years, yet while it had several severe drawbacks — it was, after all, only a modified saloon — people bought it. Lord Rootes concluded that if the company were to produce a custom-made sports car, it would find a ready market, especially in America where a larger proportion of that market existed. Accordingly, he instructed that plans be drawn up for a new sports car, a model which would embody style, comfort, and performance; a compromise maybe, but in Lord Rootes' opinion, a very acceptable one.

The man in charge of the Rootes Group's styling department at this time was Ted White. His chief appearance designer was Jeff Crompton, and he was given the task of designing a new sports car, with the specific instruction that the new model should have international appeal. Unfortunately, Crompton's first clay model was considered to be not quite right.

In 1956 Crompton was joined by an assistant called Kenneth Howes. Born in the railway town of Swindon, Howes started his career in 1940 as an apprentice in the Great Western Railway's locomotive workshops. Later, there followed a period in the London office of the stylist Raymond Loewy, and in 1952 he transferred to Loewy's New York office where he joined the design team working for Studebaker. He then moved to Ford's styling centre in Detroit where he took

The interior of Rootes' design studios. It was here that the first Alpine model was shown to Lord Rootes.

The first full-size Alpine model. Kenneth Howes was responsible for the clean lines. (Photo: Chrysler UK)

charge of the design studio. This gave Howes invaluable experience in the use of colour, texture, and large quantity production techniques. On his return to Britain in 1956 he joined the Rootes Group where he took over from Crompton the work of designing the new sports car.

Together with his assistant, Roy Axe, Howes was able to develop his own ideas. The body shape had to gain its effect from purity of sculptured form rather than rely on superfluous and ostentatious decoration. Howes started by producing a quarter-scale clay model. This was then used to develop full-scale drawings from which a full-size wooden mock-up was built. Howes had decided that the model should be painted a vivid red, a shade subsequently used on production cars, and known as Carnival Red. By December 1957, the model had been mounted on an electrically operated turntable situated at the end of the Rootes design studios, in readiness for presentation to Lord Rootes and his brother, Sir Reginald. When they saw it they were impressed. In Ted White's opinion, 80 per cent of the design was the work of Ken Howes, and 20 per cent the work of Jeff Crompton and the rest of the design team.

With the overall shape accepted, the body engineers responsible for tooling and fabrication started work on a seating buck. This took the form of a wooden platform which included floor-line, propeller shaft tunnel, dashboard and seating arrangements. From this, the designers were able to evaluate the headroom, legroom and safety factors of the new car.

To see how the new shape would behave under high-speed conditions a clay model was taken to the Motor Industry Research Association (MIRA) for wind tunnel evaluation. Body analysts had already calculated the theoretical performance data and this was compared with the measurements taken under test. With these proven correct the body engineers, under the leadership of George Payne, built metal prototypes so that a development and testing programme could begin. This programme included pavé tests (rough road), tor-

Another view of the original model. At this stage, the dashboard had yet to be finalized and resembled that of an MG TF. (Photo: Chrysler UK)

sional rigidity tests, and behaviour under crash conditions. As we shall see, the result was a body strong enough to accept far more stresses than those imposed on it by the power of the 4-cylinder engine.

In the event, only two major problems were experienced during testing: car-

The watersplash. Just one of the tests which the prototype Alpines had to undergo before production could begin. (Photo: Rolls-Royce)

buration and body vibration. The Zenith carburation expert, Charles Fisher, recalls that initially they had difficulty in aligning the inlet manifold with the alloy cylinder head and this resulted in air leaks.

One of the prototype Alpines being tested at MIRA — on pavé (rough road)... (Photo: Rolls-Royce)

... and on the banked circuit, for high-speed stability. (Photo: Rolls-Royce)

Under the bonnet of a Mk I Alpine. The strengthening stays were added to increase rigidity.

The body vibration problems were the result of too little body strength between the bulkhead and the engine compartment. Bernard Winter, head of the engineering department, took Peter Ware, engineering director, out for a demonstration drive in one of the pre-production models, and the body vibration horrified Peter Ware so much that he told Winter it would be necessary to fit strengthening stays between the bulkhead and wings. 'He was such a charming man,' recalls Ware, 'that I hated upsetting him, but I just could not allow the car to go into production like that.'

The Alpine's initial project engineer was a very experienced man called Johnny Johnson, who had been with the Singer Company for many years before Singer were taken over by Rootes. However, during a staff reorganization, Johnson was replaced by Alec Caine, who remained the Alpine's project engineer until the car's demise in 1968.

The development and testing of any new car is always a costly affair because of the considerable expenditure in time and manpower. By the time the Alpine had reached the testing stage, the Rootes engineers were heavily committed to the development of other forthcoming new models. Rather than involving them in yet another project it was decided that the Alpine's development and initial production programme should be subcontracted to Armstrong Siddeley Motors Ltd who were also in Coventry. This arrangement was not without benefit for

Kenneth Howes, the Sunbeam Alpine's designer, seen here with one of the prototypes. (Photo: K. Howes)

Armstrongs as they in turn helped develop a facsimile of the Sapphire engine for Rootes' Super Snipe.

When creating the Alpine, Rootes sought to keep costs to a minimum by utilizing as many components as possible from other models. The chassis was based on that of the Hillman Husky, a durable two-door estate car which Rootes had launched in 1955. With a wheelbase of 7 feet 2 inches (10 inches shorter than the Minx/Rapier series) the Alpine shared the same wheelbase as the Husky, but the front track was 2½ inches wider. The bodies were of monocoque construction in welded steel using the basic Husky floorpan, underbody, front and rear wheel arches. Three sub-assemblies were then welded on to this platform and together with the doors made up the complete body/chassis unit. These sub-assemblies were: the bulkhead and bonnet sides with two ties from bulkhead to wheel arches; a welded shell which formed the front wings, nose assembly and scuttle; and at the rear, a single spot-welded unit which made up the wing pressings and boot. In order to increase the strength of the original floorpan, additional cross-bracing was added on the underside.

The engine, clutch and gearbox were the same as those fitted to the Rapier, but with one main difference. The 1494 cc engine boasted a new cylinder head made of cast aluminium, which allowed for a compression ratio of 9.2:1. Twin Zenith downdraught carburettors were mounted on an alloy manifold and the power output was rated at 78 bhp at 5000 rpm. The steering mechanism consisted of a Burman recirculatory ball unit mounted high up in the engine compartment, accounting for the almost vertical steering wheel. The front suspension used coil springs with telescopic dampers and the rear suspension consisted of semi-elliptic leaf springs and lever arm dampers. The final drive operated via a Rootes-made rear axle, and a Laycock de Normanville overdrive was available as an extra.

The appearance of the new Alpine was most impressive. The low bonnet line and extended rear wings gave a pleasant wedge shape and a well-balanced overall effect.

Several features were outstanding on this new model. The two doors were particularly wide, allowing for easy access, and the hood stowage was unusually neat, the canvas resting behind three metal flaps when not in use. This undoubtedly added to the clean lines of the car when the hood was down. Wind-up windows were featured rather than the archaic sliding perspex ones often favoured by other manufacturers.

On the road the new car proved to have adequate acceleration, top speed and stopping ability. In its road test, *Autocar* commented that 'In the Alpine the needs of the sporting motorist with a young family are met. It is attractive, safe, and unquestionably fast in spite of the emphasis put on long distance comfort. The world's markets are overdue for such a car . . .'

The designers had aimed at combining good performance with comfort and clearly they had been successful. The result was not a compromise but a true dual purpose vehicle.

Motor commented, 'If this is a sports car then it belongs to a new breed of sports car which is not merely weatherproof when required, but offers two people greater comfort than they would enjoy in many quite expensive touring cars.'

Motoring correspondents invariably complimented Rootes on their attention to detail when producing a new model, and the Alpine was no exception. Selling for £971, it represented competitive rather than outstanding value. The hard top was an extra £60.

While the Alpine was a great improvement over the Mk III Sunbeam Talbot Alpine, competition from other manufacturers was still keen. The MGA, possibly the Alpine's closest rival, cost £940 and for the 1959 Motor Show, MG had made several detailed improvements to its specification — the most significant being an increase in capacity to 1588 cc. (The power output was now rated at 79.5 bhp.) Also, the front brakes had been changed to Lockheed discs. But in contrast to the Alpine, the MGA remained true to its ancestors offering minimum suspension travel combined with excellent performance and roadholding. *Autocar* described it thus: 'The MG, with its responsive engine combined with moderately heavy but low-slung chassis, adequate steering and superlative brakes, without any little vices or unpredictable traits in behaviour, maintains the tradition of the high standards of the marque.'

At the 1960 Motor Show, Rootes introduced the Alpine Mk II. Minor alterations to the rear suspension included an increase in the width of the leaf

The MGA, possibly the Alpine's closest rival during the early days. Approximately 100,000 were built between 1955 and 1962. (Photo: British Leyland)

springs and larger dampers. The engine size was increased to 1592 cc and this new 1.6 litre unit now produced 80 bhp and 94 lb/ft of torque at 3800 rpm, compared to the 89.5 lb/ft at 3400 rpm of the 1500 cc engine.

For 1961 the MGA, now known as the 1600 Mk II, was also given an increase in engine size, the new 1622 cc unit producing 90 bhp at 5500 rpm and 97 lb/ft of torque at 4000 rpm. This ostensibly small increase in engine capacity had a significant effect. The car was now forced into the 1600-2000 cc competition class and, although it was still similar in external appearance to the original 1955 model, it was now out of direct conflict with its Rootes rival.

In March 1961 the Sunbeam Harrington Alpine was introduced, built by Thomas Harrington and Company, a firm of coachbuilders in Hove, Sussex. This company had for some time pioneered the use of glass fibre in the construction of coach bodies, becoming particularly expert in the laying up and moulding of this revolutionary material. However, Harrington's considered that they were not realizing the full potential of glass fibre and, in addition, their moulding equipment was not working to full capacity. They thus decided to seek out some new project. In the event, the Harrington design team provided the answer — one which would totally involve the specialist knowledge the company had acquired. They felt that there was a market for a coach-built touring version of the Alpine — an Alpine with a fixed hard top in glass fibre. Clifford Harrington approached Alec Caine at Rootes and outlined his team's ideas. Alec was impressed, con-

Part of the Alpine production line. The complete front assembly is offered up to the body shell as it arrives on its gantry. (Photo: Rolls-Royce)

Alpine body shells about to go through the painting process. Note the high standard of cleanliness. (Photo: Rolls-Royce)

The Sunbeam Harrington Alpine. The glass fibre hard top extends from the windscreen to the rear boot. (Photo: Autocar)

sidering the new project to have distinct possibilities. (It appears that someone had criticized the size of the Alpine boot, saying flippantly that it was not large enough to accommodate a bag of golf clubs. Clearly, if the Harrington conversion overcame this particular problem, the project would be successful!)

Ron Humphries, Harrington's stylist, produced some designs from which the first moulds were built and a prototype 'hard top' was then laid up. A standard Alpine tourer was modified and fitted with the new bodywork — with impressive results, totally surpassing expectations. For this was not merely a hard top but in fact a coach-built fastback — one of the first.

Thomas Harrington Ltd (also a Rootes main vehicle distributor) had worked with Rootes for many years, using their commercial vehicle chassis and engines. Lord Rootes occasionally visited the Harrington factory in this connection, and Clifford Harrington took advantage of one such visit as an ideal opportunity to show off his new thoroughbred. When Lord Rootes arrived, Harrington guided him round the workshop and confronted him with the prototype. 'What have you been up to now?' asked Lord Rootes, yet despite this characteristic reaction, he must have been impressed, for he encouraged Harrington to proceed with development. Later, when the Harrington Alpine was formally announced in

March 1961, it was given full approval by the Rootes Group. It was available exclusively through Thomas Harrington and Company.

Shortly before the official introduction of the Harrington Alpine the Thomas Harrington Company was bought by the Robins and Day Group. This group was a private company owned by the Rootes family and run by George Hartwell who now became Harrington's new chairman. His experience was to prove invaluable in the tuning workshops, for when the Harrington Alpine was announced, among the optional extras offered were three stages of engine tune (all of which complied with FIA regulations). These tuned cars were available only through the engineering division of George Hartwell Ltd in Bournemouth. It was during this period that Desmond Rootes joined the Harrington Company, to take over the sales division.

Not long after production of the Harrington Alpine started, Rootes approached the Harrington Company with a view to modifying one of two cars they wished to enter in the 1961 Le Mans 24 hours. One of the problems for a large company such as Rootes was its inability to produce one-off prototypes conveniently. Manpower deployment and the inevitable red tape were simply not geared to low volume production and hence it was quicker, cheaper and easier for such work to

Close-up of the modified front on the Alpine Harrington Le Mans. The alterations were carried out by Harringtons in close co-operation with Rootes' design specialists. (Photo: C. Harrington)

The Harrington Alpine winning the Thermal Efficiency Index in the 1961 Le Mans. Note the large petrol filler cap projecting out of the side window. (Photo: Chrysler UK)

be effected outside the company. Harringtons agreed to prepare such a car and work began. Using a standard Sunbeam Harrington Alpine as a basis, they created a unique car, flaring the headlights into the body and fitting a large undertray beneath the front valance in an attempt to reduce drag. Luckily, the car did very well at Le Mans — much to the surprise of the Rootes Competition Team, who were in blissful ignorance of its position until John Wyer of Aston Martin came over and said, 'Hey, your car is doing well, it's winning the Thermal Efficiency Index.' Driven by Peter Proctor and Peter Harper, it covered a total distance of 2194 miles, averaging 91 mph for the 24 hours without a stop, except to take on oil, fuel and water. It finished in 16th place overall, second in the 1600 cc class to a Porsche/Abarth, and returned a higher than average speed and lower fuel consumption in terms of weight and engine capacity than any other car. Altogether, it lapped the 8.36 mile circuit 261 times and used 127.5 gallons of fuel, averaging 18 mpg. Unfortunately, the second car was disqualified.

So much interest was aroused by the Harrington race car that the company, in honour of their Le Mans achievement, introduced the Harrington Le Mans at the 1961 Motor Show. A great improvement over the Harrington Alpine GT, the new car featured a full length hard top from front windscreen to rear bumper. Access to the rear was made easy by an opening tailgate.

In order to fit this new glass fibre hard top, part of the original bodywork had to be removed and there were fears that this would cause the body to become weaker and thence to flex. A prototype was taken to the British Army's vehicle proving ground at Chobham, in Surrey and subjected to extensive testing. No major weaknesses were revealed and, with this reassuring news, it was felt safe to go ahead with manufacture. The car also boasted the following refinements: Microcell seats, veneered dashboard, special wood-rimmed steering wheel, oil cooler, brake servo, competition clutch, and an engine tuned by George Hartwell to give 104 bhp at 6000 rpm. The result was a handsome, well equipped GT car, priced at £1495.

Harringtons had intended to introduce a third series of hard top. Like the series I, it would have required few body modifications, but would have featured the opening tailgate of the series II. In the event, only a handful of hard tops were made before production finally stopped. The price of the complete car was to have been £1196.

The decision to terminate construction of the Harrington Alpine was the result of a company policy meeting. The Harrington coachbuilding company, responsible for the construction of coach and motor bodies, utilized non-mass production

The Sunbeam Alpine Harrington Le Mans, from this view looking somewhat similar to the Mk III Triumph GT6. The car was introduced in 1962, in honour of the Harrington Alpine's performance at Le Mans the previous year.

The Harrington Alpine type C, seen here outside the Harrington factory in Hove. This hard top benefited from the opening tailgate of the Le Mans, yet did not require such extensive modifications. (Photo: C. Harrington)

techniques and it was decided to redirect their efforts into the Rootes franchise. Unfortunately, factory records giving accurate production figures have long since been destroyed, but it is thought that approximately 150 Harrington Alpine GTs were produced together with 250 or more Harrington Le Mans.

In November 1961, following Stirling Moss and Jack Brabham's success in an Alpine at Riverside Raceway, California, Rootes agents in the western states of America sold their entire stock of Alpines, and sales for the car in the forthcoming year were forecast to be £7 million.

But despite the Alpine's apparent success, it still had several shortcomings. Rootes themselves were aware of these and the car's project engineer, Alec Caine, was constantly thinking of ways to improve it. He drew up several plans for modifying the boot to provide greater space but as with the Harrington Le Mans project, the problem was in arranging for this development work to be carried out. However, a lucky opportunity presented itself when it became known that one of Rootes' Italian dealers owed the company some money. Rather than pursuing the debt, it was decided that the dealer should finance whatever modifications would be required and have them carried out by Carozzeria

Superleggera Touring of Milan. Once the arrangements were made, Alec Caine set out for Italy in an Alpine one Friday evening. After only one week's work, the job was complete and he returned with two new wing fuel tanks and the spare wheel moved to a vertical position in the boot. This increased the boot capacity enormously and the modification was later included on production models.

In an attempt to make the series II Alpine more competitive, Rootes decided to offer a comprehensive selection of tuning parts (to attract the performance seekers) which were to be made available through spare parts stockists. To this end Jack Brabham was asked to develop a special Alpine which could be evaluated by the Rootes engineers. Unfortunately, the car was not completely successful under test, and so Rootes went ahead and manufactured their own tuning equipment and published a tuning guide: *The Sunbeam Alpine Series II Special Tuning.* Brabham, meanwhile, offered his own conversion for the Alpine separately.

By 1962, space had been found at Rootes' Ryton-on-Dunsmore plant and production of the Alpine was transferred from Armstrong's Parkside factory.

The Mk III Alpine was introduced at the Geneva Motor Show in March 1963. In addition to many worthwhile improvements to the open car, a GT model was also offered. The GT had a revised style of removable hard top which was more angular in shape than the earlier version, and in order to create the best styling effect when it was in position, Rootes had redesigned the doors, giving the leading edges square corners in place of round ones. Early owners had complained of a condition called 'Alpine neck', caused by draughts created by the original hard top. It was hoped that the new hard top would solve the problem. Alec Caine's rearrangement of the boot area with the twin rear tanks increased the fuel capacity to 11.25 gallons. Rootes recognized the potential mood of the GT by making the whole car quieter. This was achieved by fitting a twin-choke Solex carburettor fed through a large air cleaner, in place of the twin downdraughts of the tourer. However, this positive reduction in noise level lost the engine some 7 bhp which it could hardly afford. Other alterations included a change from a crossflow to a vertical flow radiator with integral header tank, a gearbox with revised ratios, telescopic rear dampers, a reinforced front cross-member, a larger diameter anti-roll bar, and an increase in the size of the front disc diameter. A vacuum servo was also standard on both models. A novel feature, also developed by Alec Caine, was the adjustable steering column. Merely by turning the steering wheel boss a half turn, the driver could move the wheel backwards or forwards by as much as 2½ inches. The clutch and brake pedal positions could also be adjusted. Both the soft top and the revised style hard top gave an extra 1 inch headroom. The price of the tourer was £840, while the GT cost £60 more.

With the introduction of the GT, potential customers had an awkward choice. The roadster was supplied with a soft top as standard equipment; the GT was not. So although a hard top bought as an extra could be fitted to the open (and cheaper) car, owners of the GT had but one choice of weather protection. On the

The Alpine Mk III in both Tourer and GT form. While a hard top was available as an extra for the Tourer, there was no soft top alternative for the GT. (Photo: Autocar)

other hand, the GT did benefit from the extra space behind the seats, in the rear.

Autocar commented, 'What the new car may lack in punch, it makes up for in relative quietness of its progress: and one must admire its good looks.'

Certainly, the Alpine was developing a reputation for excellent ride, finish and finesse. The only penalty was a lack of performance.

By 1963 the MGA had been superceded. Its successor, the MGB, was generally considered to be a superior car with a larger engine, wind-up windows, and a far better ride. 14 inch wheels replaced the earlier 15 inch fitted to the MGA, and not long after its introduction, overdrive was made available as an extra. The 1798 cc engine developed 95.6 bhp at 5400 rpm and 100 lb/ft of torque at 3000 rpm. Its price was a competitive £847.

However, the traditional open sports car now seemed to be entering a new phase. The emphasis was less on soft tops and more on heaters and hard tops. As the roads became more crowded, so a ride in an open sports car, with the inevitable smell of exhaust fumes, became less pleasureable. Also, statistics indicated that people were getting married earlier, which in turn was creating a market for sporting saloons, more suited to the young family man. Cars such as the Mini Cooper 1275 S costing £755 and the four-door Ford Cortina GT costing £780 offered near equal performance yet greater seating capacity.

When the Alpine was introduced in 1959, its wedge shape was generally thought to be very pleasing, but as styles changed so the pronounced fins became dated. Inevitably, this led Rootes' stylists to redesign the rear wing section, the new shape closely following the lines of the Hillman Minx saloon. During this period, Rootes signed a direct contract with Touring of Milan. The contract concerned the assembly of the Alpine for the Italian market, and the manufacture of a coupé version of the Sceptre, called the Venezia. In early November 1963, Touring exhibited an Alpine with the newly styled rear section at the Turin Motor Show.

Rootes displayed the new Mk IV Alpine at the Brussels Motor Show in January 1964. This latest Alpine embodied the same major restyling first seen on

Rootes' revised treatment of the rear wings, seen here on the Superleggera Alpine. These alterations were later introduced on the Mk IV Alpine. (Photo: Autocar)

the Italian car two months earlier. The rear fins had been cut off vertically, giving the car a more taut, compact look. Minor alterations included a single chrome strip across the front of the radiator, replacing the previous four bar type, and a veneered dashboard was fitted to the GT. An automatic version was also offered which, Rootes claimed, was the first automatic sports car to be imported into the United States. John Panks, the director of Rootes Motors Incorporated (America), said it was expected that the addition of an automatic version would increase the company's sales in the States from between 35 to 50 per cent and would be especially attractive to Americans in the 18-30 year age group who had little experience of gear changing. The prices of the new cars were: Tourer, £853; GT, £914; Automatic Alpine, £1004.

On the mechanical side, the GT and the roadster shared identical engines, both being fitted with the single twin-choke carburettor, which produced 82 bhp at 5000 rpm and 93 lb/ft of torque at 3500 rpm. By now some American States had introduced legislation against pollution, and the new engine had been modified to comply with the EPA regulations. Anti-fade dampers were fitted to the suspension and the spring rates were reduced to give a better ride. The Mk IV was the best so far. A car with panache, it appealed to customers on both sides of the Atlantic.

Unfortunately, while Rootes continued to produce cars of good quality (the Alpine amongst them), the company's financial position was deteriorating. A strike involving British Light Steel Pressings at Acton in London had drained Rootes of vital financial resources. By the time the company had resumed production, Rootes' profits were not sufficient to fund the development of much needed new models. In addition, the steady increase in the cost of raw materials, together with an upwards wages spiral, was taking its toll. The development programme and tooling costs for the Hillman Imp also weighed heavily upon the company's budget. Rootes' salvation came in the form of an agreement with Chrysler (America), finalized in June 1964, which gained the group £12 million of Chrysler finance, plus a £15 million rights issue underwritten by Chrysler. While Lord Rootes insisted that the new deal should be considered as a marriage of the two companies, the cost of the matrimony had set Chrysler back nearly $35 million.

In fact, this new link was a renewal of old acquaintances, for in earlier years Rootes had been a distributor for the Maxwell Company, the forerunner of the Chrysler Corporation. Under the terms of the 1964 agreement, the manufacturing, engineering and sales techniques of each company could be shared to mutual advantage. In reality, this advantage tended to weigh more heavily in Rootes' favour, for from this point on stylists in Chrysler's Detroit studios began sending design suggestions to their opposite numbers in Coventry. The major benefit to Chrysler, of course, was that they now gained a badly needed foothold in the British market.

In October 1964, Rootes made a significant improvement to the Alpine when they introduced an all synchromesh gearbox. This overcame a long-standing criticism of the car, and the opportunity was also taken to alter the body slightly. The trailing edges of the doors and bonnet were given rectangular corners.

The Mk V Alpine was the last of the line. Introduced in September 1965, the hood stowage was altered, the design incorporating a vinyl bag which held the hood when not in use. The boot edges were square-cornered and additional air vents positioned in the footwells assisted ventilation. On the mechanical side, an alternator replaced the dynamo. To overcome the fussiness of the Mk IV engine, the Mk V featured a five-bearing crankshaft which, with an increased throw, brought the capacity to 1725 cc. Two Stromberg carburettors replaced the twin choke Solex and, as a result, the power output was increased to 98.5 bhp and torque was 110 lb/ft at 3700 rpm. Rootes had obviously done their homework for the engine was now much smoother and petrol consumption, especially with the overdrive, was considered good for its day. *Autocar* was impressed: 'No one seriously expects sports cars to be draughty, noisy and uncomfortable these days. Complete weather protection, comfortable seats and adequate luggage room with docile manners, and close on 100 mph are now demanded by the enthusiast. The Alpine V provides all these and although it's approaching its seventh birthday,

The engine compartment of the Mk V Alpine. Stromberg carburettors replaced the twin choke Solex and the power was increased to 98.5 bhp. (Photo: Autocar)

continual improvements in equipment and power output have maintained its competitive position.' The price of the Alpine remained competitive too, with the Tourer at £893 and the GT at £954.

In tracing the Alpine's history we have been able to see how the car was gradually developed from its initial introduction in 1959. Rootes finally terminated production in January 1968 — thereby relinquishing all ties with the sports car market. Providing as it did comfortable, open-air motoring, the car always lacked performance. This fact did not escape the Rootes family, and as early as 1961 means of increasing the performance had been considered. John Panks, for example, had several meetings with the Rootes board and suggestions such as the possible use of the Humber Hawk engine had been discussed. In the event, two other units were tried. Don Tarbun (a member of Rootes' development department) recalls, 'We were given the opportunity to install either the four cylinder 1600 cc Alfa Romeo engine or the Daimler 2½ litre V8 unit, with the explicit instructions that the substitute engine had to be fitted with the minimum of body modifications. Alas, neither unit proved satisfactory and the idea was dropped.'

In the early sixties, Jack Brabham, too, had ideas for vastly improving the Alpine's performance. His workshops were already involved in the production of tuning kits for the Alpine but, like Rootes' development department, Brabham realized that the only real way to increase the Alpine's performance was to install a larger engine. To this end, he had several discussions with Rootes representatives and in particular, Peter Ware, suggesting the installation of an American V8 engine. However, as Brabham remembers, 'They were listening but seemed embarrassed at the idea of an American engine in one of their cars.'

Brabham is honest enough to admit that he was hoping Rootes would agree to his Alpine V8 ideas because of the inevitable increase in work this would give his engineering business. 'We had the manpower and knowhow,' he continued, 'and could have undertaken series production modifying standard Alpines and fitting V8 engines.'

The proposed American Ford unit measured just 20 inches (508mm) across the cylinder banks whereas the Daimler engine was over 28 inches (711.2mm) and had a rear mounted distributor. This accounted for the difficulty Rootes' development department had in installing the Daimler engine into the Alpine.

When reflecting on the Alpine's development, it is interesting to note how Rootes were influenced from outside. The Alpine Harrington Le Mans with its luxurious appointments must have induced Rootes to develop their own GT soon after. The major body restyling, too, which resulted in the Mk IV Alpine, further illustrates how responsive the Rootes design team were to outside changes in style.

It was yet another outside involvement which turned the Alpine into the Tiger.

A Mk I Tiger. The owner has gone to great lengths to maintain the car in its original condition.

Steve Strong's 'Harrington' Tiger. This car features a Harrington type C hard top.

Ford to the Rescue

There have been many attempts to install large V8 American engines into European cars in the pursuit of extra performance, for the art of engine swopping or 'shoehorning' is far from new. Of these, surely, Carroll Shelby's AC Cobra must remain the most celebrated. By 1963, the Cobra had already gained an enviable reputation both on the road and on the racetrack as a successful Anglo-American amalgamation and it was this formula together with Shelby's highly skilled workforce which was crucial to the Tiger's development.

Born in Leesburg, Texas, Shelby had a successful but varied racing career. In 1956 he was nominated American Driver of the Year by *Sports Illustrated* magazine, and in 1959 he and Roy Salvadori won the Le Mans 24 hours driving an Aston Martin DBR1/300, perhaps his best known win. The following year, Shelby was nominated USAC champion. Sadly, his racing career was abruptly halted as a result of a deteriorating heart condition, but his retirement from active racing was not without irony. Shelby now had the time to realize a personal ambition: to build a superlative open sports car. The car of his dreams was to be similar in concept to the big Austin Healey but powered by an American V8 engine. The major consideration was to find a suitable body/chassis unit and events were to lead Shelby to select the AC Ace.

For many years, AC's Thames Ditton factory had used the Bristol 2 litre, 6 cylinder engine in their sports cars. Although an excellent engine, it did require skilled use of the gearbox in order to derive the best performance from it. Bristol's competitors, however, manufacturers of high-quality, low volume, performance cars, were slowly changing to larger engines coupled to automatic transmissions. Unfortunately, Bristol's own engine did not lend itself to automatic changes and so the company sought an alternative power unit. This they found in Chrysler's 313 cu in, 5113 cc V8, thereupon ceasing production of their own engine in 1959. AC had sensibly stockpiled a large quantity of Bristol engines, thus enabling production to continue, but they realized that a replacement unit had to be found eventually.

Ken Rudd, a garage owner in Worthing, Sussex, had experimented earlier by replacing the Bristol engine with the British Ford (Zephyr) 6 cylinder unit. AC were so impressed with the result that they decided to approach Ford at Dagenham for a contract for the supply of these engines. Ford immediately agreed. Unfortunately, sales of ACs began to drop when fitted with the replacement power unit. The buying public maintained that the Bristol engine was irreplaceable, and AC's future looked very bleak. When Shelby heard of AC's predicament, he immediately realized the opportunities open to him and wrote to the Thames Ditton factory, outlining his general ideas and asking for their co-operation. As he later said, 'I decided I had better get going, but quick, before the AC factory decided to close down altogether.' However, AC replied favourably. Now all that Shelby needed to complete his ideal sports car was a suitable power unit.

A chance meeting between Shelby and Dave Evans, then in charge of the engine department of Ford's (America) stock car racing team, subsequently provided Shelby with the engines he required. Shelby explained to Evans his theory on mating an American V8 engine with the AC chassis. Evans then told Shelby of a new lightweight engine which Ford had recently developed. He offered Shelby two of the new 221 cu in (3.6-litre) engines and arranged to have them delivered to Shelby's workshops in Santa Fe Springs. Not long after, Evans contacted Shelby offering him two of the high performance 260 cu in (4.2-litre) engines. Immediately, one of the larger units was sent over to Thames Ditton, followed soon after by Shelby himself.

These lightweight, compact engines (which subsequently proved crucial to the Alpine V8 project) were the result of Ford's intense interest in the hot rod and stock car craze of the 1950s, and were the culmination of three years' research and development by Robert Stirrat. Stirrat started work on the Ford lightweight unit in 1958, his main objective being to produce a cast iron engine which would compare favourably in weight with an equivalent unit made of alloy. Although Ford had made alloy engines in the past, they considered that the benefit in weight reduction did not justify the cost. So the company decided to pursue development using cast iron, a material they knew to have certain advantages. For example, because its graphite content is an integral part of its molecular structure, it serves to act as a lubricant while its thermal expansion characteristics are nearly ideal at all operating temperatures (assuming the engine has the correct clearances). Additional benefits in using cast iron are the sound deadening qualities and its ability to dampen vibration. The design of the cylinder block was checked by using stress-coating techniques which involved painting the block with a special liquid and subjecting it to stress. By studying the stress lines with stroboscopic light, the engineers were able to see exactly which areas required extra strengthening.

Stirrat was aided in his development of a lighter engine by Ford's latest foundry techniques, in particular, 'thin-wall casting'. In developing this new technique, Ford sought to overcome the necessity of producing over-thick wall sections in their engines simply to account for casting fluctuations. In some cases, these fluctuations were considerable and the thickness was merely to maintain strength. Where there was a lack of fluidity in the molten iron, thicker sections were required to prevent 'blow-holes' and 'chilling'. Also, in any casting process, there is a certain amount of rough surfaces and to allow for this, the casting thickness must necessarily be made thicker. Aside from being very wasteful in material, all this combined to make the engines much heavier.

Several techniques were developed to overcome these problems. For example, cores were made hollow using plastic resin, binders were added to the sand and quick baking was adopted using pre-heated core boxes. Removing the cores from the boxes always gave distortion but by using redesigned cores, fewer were used which resulted in less shifting at the connecting sections. Also, cores were coated to give a smoother surface and a higher ramming force was used to push the sand further into the mould — techniques which gave cleaner cast faces.

The aim was a weight reduction of between 25 and 30 per cent for a given engine size. Apart from the obvious saving in materials, 'thin-wall casting' helped reduce 'dead' weight — one of the biggest enemies of performance cars.

Stirrat introduced other features on this engine. The V8 arrangement allowed all-round water jacketing of each cylinder, the water space being continued right down to the base of the cylinder block. However, because of the compact dimensions of the engine, there was insufficient room inside the crankcase for the crankshaft balance weights. To maintain total balance, external counter-weights were fitted, one on the flywheel and one on the extension of the crankshaft outside the timing case.

Initially, these engines were of 221 cu in (3621 cc) displacement but soon after their introduction a high performance version became available. Of 260 cu in (4261 cc) this unit developed 164 bhp at 4400 rpm and produced a healthy 258 lb/ft of torque at 2200 rpm. The combustion chambers were wedge shaped and the aluminiumized valves were inclined and operated via self-adjusting hydraulic tappets. A two barrel carburretor mounted on a cast iron manifold situated centrally between the cylinder heads fed the separate inlet ports.

Stirrat's efforts produced an engine which was both light in weight and compact in size: it weighed 450 lb (204 kg) and the block measured 8.93 inches (226.8 mm) high, 16.36 inches (415.5 mm) wide and 20.48 inches (529.3 mm) long. Its state of tune resulted in a very unstressed unit and because the power was developed at such low revs it was unnecessary, even undesirable, to exceed 5000 rpm.

By the time Shelby arrived in England, work had already started on the new V8 powered AC. Although fitting the larger engine into the AC body presented no problems, the chassis required modifying to accept the greater power. The rear differential carrier was strengthened together with the front suspension. Also, the spring hangers and stub axles were redesigned. The original Tojeiro transverse leaf sprung chassis had just never been expected to take such potential punishment, as the 2-litre Bristol engine developed only 125 bhp.

The first car was called CSX 0001, standing for Carroll Shelby Experimental. On 20 February 1962, it left Thames Ditton to be flown back to California. When it arrived, Shelby rang Dave Evans at Ford and explained what progress

The chassis of an early AC Cobra. The transverse leaf springs are clearly visible. (Photo: B. Fone)

had been made. Evans was impressed and invited Shelby to come up to the factory for a meeting with Don Frey, who at the time was in charge of development strategy. The result of the meeting was an agreement to supply Shelby with engines. With a similar agreement from AC to supply the body/chassis units, Shelby was in a position to begin building cars.

CSX 0001 was exhibited at the New York Motor Show in 1962 under its production name of AC Cobra. The car was to be built in left-hand drive form only and was designated immediately into the SCCA Class 'A' production category for racing. The AC Ace's styling was left unaltered except for the addition of small lips over the wheel arches to cover the wide-section tyres. The engine was coupled to a Borg-Warner four-speed all synchromesh gearbox which in turn drove a Salisbury differential. 12 inch Girling disc brakes were fitted all round and (depending on the state of tune) Shelby claimed a top speed of over 150 mph. Only the initial 75 cars were fitted with the 260 cu in (4.2 litre) engines for in the spring of 1964, Ford introduced a more powerful engine of 289 cu in (4.7 litres) which was then substituted for the original unit.

A left-hand drive '260' AC Cobra tested by John Bolster for *High Performance Cars* was very highly praised for both its engine and roadholding. 'It is literally smooth up to 6500 rpm and would go higher if one turned a blind eye to the rev counter', commented Bolster. 'At fast cornering speeds the Cobra is easy to handle but driven to the limit it is not a car for the beginner. The AC Cobra', he concluded, 'is a high quality sports car with stupendous performance.'

On 19 July 1962, the second experimental car, CSX 0002, was despatched to America where in October, driven by Ken Miles at Riverside Raceway, it made its racing debut. Unfortunately, the car retired with a broken hub.

By early 1963, production of Cobras had started and Shelby entered a car in the 1963 Le Mans 24 Hours. Fitted with a racing 4.7 engine, it was timed at over 160 mph down the Mulsanne straight and finished seventh overall. In 1964, Shelby's cars all but won the FIA GT World Championship: the 6 hour Monza race due to be held on 6 September that year was cancelled, and this probably cost Shelby the Championship. As it was, he won the US Road Racing Championship instead.

In America, the early 1960s were probably the heyday for imported sports cars. European manufacturers such as MG, Triumph, and Porsche, were well aware that to be really successful at selling their sports cars, they had to be competitive on the race track. Equally, American manufacturers — Ford and General Motors in particular — saw the youth market as a potential money-spinner and began aiming some of their models at this section of the motoring public. In this respect too Shelby was very successful — the amalgamation of the V8 engine and the lightweight body was working; his cars were becoming invincible on the race track and as a result, sales were increasing dramatically.

Ian Garrad, Rootes' West Coast manager, could hardly fail to notice the

The AC Cobra with its creator, Carroll Shelby. Depending on engine tune, the car was capable of 175 mph. (Photo: Shelby American Automobile Club)

Ian Garrad, at the wheel of a Tiger. The project owed a great deal to his foresight and enthusiasm.

interest being shown by other manufacturers in the high performance and youth market, and was well aware of the Sunbeam Alpine's limited attraction in a field where performance and cubic capacity were of primary importance. Garrad concluded that what was needed was a new model, a sports car with sufficient power to compete with E types, Healeys and Porsches on their own terms.

As the son of Norman Garrad, Rootes' competitions manager, Ian was no doubt well aware of Rootes' early attempts at uprating the Alpine and in particular, the suggestions put forward by Jack Brabham concerning the installation of a Ford V8 engine. At the beginning of 1963, as a spectator at many of the race meetings where Shelby's Cobras were so successful, Brabham clearly remembers having several meetings with Garrad, discussing a solution to the Alpine's lack of performance and the installation of a V8 engine. Garrad put these ideas to his friend Doane Spencer, of Hollywood Sports Cars, suggesting that the 216 cu in (3.5 litre) Buick/Oldsmobile engine might possibly fit the bill. Spencer was less enthusiastic. 'Forget those engines,' he told Garrad, 'they're bigger than the car itself. Use a Ford unit.' As Spencer later admitted, 'I had installed several of these Buick engines in MGs and while the unit is very light (only 325lb) it would not have been suitable for the Alpine as it is too wide. Anyway, in suggesting the Ford engine I had hoped to get the job of fitting one into the Alpine myself, but as it turned out, the project went to Shelby.'

In fact, General Motors produced only 750,000 of the 3.5 litre alloy V8 engines before production was terminated in late 1963, to make way for the development of larger cast iron units. As no suitable unit was available from the Chrysler Corporation itself, Garrad had little hesitation in choosing the Ford V8 unit as being the most suited to the Alpine's bodyshell. Ironically, by so doing, he had already determined the Tiger's short life.

Garrad now telephoned his boss in New York, John Panks, director of Rootes Motors Inc, America, and explained his proposals. Panks immediately grasped the implications of such a modification and within two days had flown over from his office in New York to Los Angeles for further discussions with Garrad.

Panks's arrival coincided with the 1963 Grand Prix at Riverside Raceway, where an Alpine competing in Class F Production finished third overall in the main event. This result, indicating the Alpine's chassis potential but once again underlining its lack of performance, convinced Panks of Garrad's arguments. At a dinner later that evening, the two men met Shelby. Not unnaturally, the main topic of conversation was the success of the Cobra and the possibility of adapting the same 'shoehorn' technique for the Alpine. They also talked of the sales success in the States of the Chevrolet Corvette, the E-type Jaguar and the Austin Healey, which were all outselling the Alpine by a long way. Shelby, obviously equating the Alpine with the AC Cobra, suggested installing a Ford V8 engine. He pointed out the advantages of a lightweight, high performance engine in a small car, and proceeded to explain how he thought the job could be done. Later that evening further discussions were held between the two Rootes executives in Panks's hotel.

The next step was to see if the engine would fit, and the following Sunday Panks, Garrad and Ken Miles (Shelby's chief development engineer and test driver) met at Shelby's workshop in Venice, Los Angeles. The three men proceeded to chalk out on the floor the relative dimensions of the engine and car. A quick appraisal revealed that it might just work. Panks and Garrad went back to their office and discussed the implications. If the engine could be fitted into the Alpine, and if the Rootes board in England could be persuaded to accept the idea, then they just might be in business. First they had to arrange for a prototype to be built.

At this point they decided to take Brian Rootes into their confidence. As Brian was visiting San Francisco, Ian flew up for a meeting. During a heavy drinking session in a waterfront bar, he explained his proposals. Brian was fascinated by the project and told Ian to proceed. Armed with such reassuring support, Panks instructed Garrard to commission Carroll Shelby to build a prototype car and to pay for it out of the advertising budget. Shelby agreed to accept the project, charging $10,000 for the work plus a commission on each car that was subsequently sold. 'It'll be ready in about eight weeks' time', he told Garrad. 'Eight weeks,' thought Garrad, 'I can't wait that long.' So he contacted Ken Miles and asked him if he would perform a quick engine swop. Miles agreed, saying that he could do the job for around $600. Although he was actually employed by Shelby at that time, Ken Miles had his own workshop and it was here that the first prototype was built.

In March 1963 a Mk II Alpine was delivered to the Miles workshop and work began. The scuttle was left unaltered, as were the steering, suspension, and rear

The first Alpine to be fitted with a Ford V8 engine. It was built by Ken Miles, who made every effort to make it look as original as possible. Resprayed candy apple red, it had automatic transmission and covered approximately 5000 miles in two weeks. Note the alloy wheels. (Photos: Ian Garrad)

axle. As Miles was unable to obtain a manual Ford gearbox, the 260 cu in (4.2-litre) engine was fitted with a two-speed automatic transmission. Care was taken to ensure that the car's external appearance was normal — even the exhaust system appeared original with just one pipe protruding from the rear. Inside, only the addition of a Sun tachometer and an automatic gear selector gave any clue to what lay beneath the bonnet. The result was somewhat of a handful. The engine, mounted as far forward as possible, made the car very nose heavy, and the narrow wheels had great difficulty in transmitting the power to the road. Resprayed candy apple red, the car was at first fitted with wire wheels, but these were soon replaced by cast alloy wheels when it was found that the spokes could not handle the power.

Initially, trouble was experienced with cooling. Lack of room had prevented the normal fan from being fitted and so Miles had fabricated mountings in front of the radiator to take Jaguar electric fans. This arrangement proved unsatisfactory and there was a delay while a larger size radiator was hunted down and installed. Nevertheless, within a week, the car was running. In John Panks's words, 'After three weeks of work we still had a lash-up, but after six weeks we had the makings of a very nice motor car.'

Unfortunately, when the real testing began, many problems emerged. The rear axle ratio was incorrect, the rear leaf springs wound up under fierce acceleration, and instability set in at high speed due to adverse weight distribution. However, with Miles's immense experience, many of these faults were corrected. A rack and pinion steering unit found in a breaker's yard was fitted and this allowed the

engine to be moved further back in the body shell, improving the handling enormously. Top speed and acceleration were more than sufficient to prove the validity of Ian's theory and in a little over two weeks the car covered 5000 miles, including two days' driving up and down the hills of San Francisco and several high speed runs along the West Coast.

Meanwhile, Shelby's team had completed the second prototype. When asked to describe the work done by his team in developing this car, Shelby is a little reticent, but this is perhaps understandable as it was, in the words of one of his employees, a 'cut and fit or cut and try and fit operation'.

As is so often the case with such jobs, the whole project was started and completed without the aid of diagrams or notes. In mid-April a white Alpine was delivered to Shelby's Venice workshops and the team started work. A standard 260 cu in (4.2 litre) engine, with 'stock' clutch and manual gearbox, was fitted and the required modifications were made to the chassis and engine compartment. A special propeller shaft was made to transmit the power to the modified Ford Galaxie final drive unit.

In order to position the engine as far back in the engine compartment as possible, Shelby's team tried a worm and sector steering layout (as used in the early Cobras). 'But they came up against some snags,' recalls Doane Spencer, 'so I suggested a rack and pinion unit and gave them an MG rack from my workshop.' It was obvious that the Rootes radiator would not be adequate for the larger engine and so a foreshortened American Ford version was installed.

The two men who deserve recognition for the job of building this second V8

The Shelby-built prototype which was demonstrated to Lord Rootes in Coventry. It was later returned to America and disappeared for many years, before turning up in southern California.

Alpine are George Boskoff as head mechanic, and Phil Remington as chief engineer, although at the time Remington was still heavily involved in the Shelby racing programme and much of the work was left to Boskoff.

When Remington and Boskoff had finished, Garrad was given a demonstration. One problem immediately became apparent: the final drive ratios were unsuitable. Further development was clearly required and the car was taken to Doane Spencer at Hollywood Sports Cars for modification. Spencer replaced the somewhat stout Ford Galaxie final drive with a Studebaker Champion unit. With this work completed, the suspension had to be adjusted and so Ken Miles, Shelby's chief test engineer, took the car to Riverside Raceway for handling evaluation. A rigorous test schedule then followed, ranging from journeys through heavy Los Angeles traffic to crossing the Mojave Desert where temperatures often exceed 100°F.

The tests completed, and the cars finally proved, Panks and Garrad reflected on the situation. Without doubt the cars were quick — very quick, considering what had been done — and the results were as good as they had hoped for. The cost had been minimal and, while they had none of the experimental road test reports or engineering drawings normally associated with a new development which could be used for reference purposes at a later date, they did have the actual cars. The only problem now was to convince the Rootes family that the project was a viable proposition.

John Panks, director of Rootes Motors Inc at the time of the Tiger project.

Briefly, the specification for each car was as follows:

Miles-built car: 4.2 litre engine; automatic transmission; standard Alpine steering, brakes, and final drive; red bodyshell.

Shelby-built car: 4.2 litre engine; manual transmission; modified steering using MG steering rack, Studebaker Champion final drive; white bodyshell.

While the Miles-built car was probably faster on acceleration, its handling was lethal as a result of its very nose-heavy attitude. In addition, the speed with which the engine change was completed was reflected in the standard of workmanship. The Shelby car had a higher maximum speed and far better handling, due to the fact that the engine had been located farther back in the body. Thus, while the Miles-built car had clearly proven the theory, the Shelby car was chosen to sell the idea to the Rootes family, as originally planned.

Panks now telephoned Lord Rootes in Coventry and explained what they had just done. His reaction was characteristic: 'What the hell have you been up to?', he demanded. 'Don't prejudge me or prejudge the car', retorted Panks, going on to ask if Lord Rootes could arrange to receive Ian Garrad at Coventry when he brought the car over. Now all that remained was for the car to prove itself to the company. Although unbaptized, the Tiger was, at least, born.

Demonstrations and Decisions

On a sunny day in July 1963, a banana boat docked at Southampton carrying a rather special cargo. For in addition to fruit, the vessel brought the Shelby-prepared V8 Alpine, on its way from Los Angeles to Coventry. The car had been driven from California across America to New York by Mrs Zymalski, wife of Ed Zymalski, Rootes' regional manager for Chicago. Here it had been placed on board the boat en route for England — this, in John Panks's opinion, being the most economical way of transporting it.

Somewhat unceremoniously, it was dumped on the quayside to await collection. Meanwhile, Ian Garrad had flown from Los Angeles to London, and travelled down to Southampton with his brother Lewis, also an employee of Rootes. After completing the formalities, they filled the car up with petrol and began the last leg of the journey to Rootes' headquarters in Coventry.

On arrival, Ian and Lewis drove directly to Rootes' Ryton factory. After parking in the visitors' car park, they went off to report to Peter Ware, now engineering director. However, Ware declined their invitation to view the car, suggesting instead that they visit the Stoke factory further into Coventry and demonstrate it to his assistant, Peter Wilson. So Lewis and Ian motored along to the Stoke plant on Humber Road, in search of Peter Wilson.

Possibly remembering some of the less complimentary things that had been said in the past about American 'shoehorn' conversions, it was with some reservation that Wilson walked out into the summer sunshine to view Garrad's pride

Peter Wilson, the first man at Coventry to drive the Shelby prototype brought over by Ian Garrad.

and joy. Deliberately refraining from making any premature comments, he walked round the car and climbed into the left-hand driving seat for a trial run. He lit his pipe and started the engine, engaged first gear, and moved slowly out into Humber Road. By the time he had sampled the acceleration in second gear, his pipe had gone out and he was gripping the wheel excitedly. A change up to third jerked his pipe to the floor where it remained for the rest of the journey.

Wilson was exuberant and went off to report to Peter Ware. Garrad breathed a sigh of relief; the initial hurdle was over. As requested by John Panks, Lord Rootes had arranged to be at the factory to take a test drive, and some members of the Rootes board, including Geoffrey and Timothy Rootes and Peter Ware, gathered to watch as he took the wheel. The chairman's decision to drive the car himself was certainly unusual in view of his limited driving experience, for in latter years he had been chauffeur-driven almost everywhere. As he drove away in perhaps the fastest car he had ever handled, Geoffrey Rootes remarked, 'I hope he doesn't do anything bloody silly.' He did.

When a smiling Lord Rootes returned, the car was enveloped in a pungent,

Sir Geoffrey and Lord William Rootes with HRH Prince Philip and Peter Ware at a Linwood function.

burning smell. The cause of the trouble was soon located: he had made the entire journey with the handbrake on!

Lord Rootes was clearly impressed (in spite of the handbrake), and he had good reason to be optimistic about the car's potential. It can be supposed that he considered the car's American engine to be a major marketing advantage. The sales of any high performance car were likely to be greatest in the United States, and the problem of spares and servicing for this Alpine variation would thus be largely overcome.

So enthusiastic was Lord Rootes that he immediately set about contacting Henry Ford to arrange for the purchase of V8 engines himself. Telephoning Henry Ford proved a little difficult but he was finally located sunbathing on a yacht in the Bahamas. Lord Rootes outlined his plans and requested the initial purchase of some 400 units. Ford did not make an immediate decision but instead contacted Lee Anthony Iacocca, his executive vice president in charge of sales. Iacocca was very critical of the suggested deal. His argument was that the Mustang — Ford's own 'sports coupé' — had been developed for the youth market, and that the V8-engined Alpine would thus conflict with Ford's marketing interests.

At this stage John Panks was called in as arbitrator, and he went to Detroit to negotiate on behalf of Lord Rootes, the subsequent discussions taking up a considerable amount of his time. He explained that according to Rootes' most ambitious forecasts, sales of the Alpine V8 were not expected to exceed 8000 units per year. Iacocca still feared that the British car might have an adverse effect on Mustang sales, especially if it was backed up by a strong advertising campaign. In retrospect, this reaction is difficult to understand for when the Mustang was launched, the motoring magazines reported that Iacocca saw it essentially as a four-seater family car, albeit one with a sporting performance. In contrast, the Alpine V8 was a high performance, two-seater sports car, and not in any way a family car. However, the Mustang was very much Iacocca's brain child (he was known throughout Ford, Detroit as 'Mr Mustang'), and he may well have been hyper-sensitive about any possible competition. Once he fully appreciated the situation, negotiations proceeded more favourably — in fact, Panks remembers that both Henry Ford and Lee Iacocca demonstrated 'a complete understanding of what our objectives were and wanted to help as much as they could.'

By mid-November 1963, negotiations between Ford and Rootes had been completed, and the first fifty engines were on their way to Britain. The contract called for the delivery of 300 power units per month at a reputed cost of approximately $600 each.

Lord Rootes gave the design team specific instructions for minimal external alterations. As we shall see, this concept of the car, as a wolf in sheep's clothing, was to prove fairly contentious later on. Almost immediately, the project ran into problems, concerning building space, manpower and developmental techniques. Peter Wilson recalls: 'As soon as it became apparent that Rootes were to build this new model, we had to decide who was to be responsible for undertaking the work. At that time Rootes had neither the space nor the experienced manpower to take on the project, so it was decided to sub-contract the work to Jensen at West Bromwich. Several factors influenced this choice, possibly the most important being the experience the Jensen engineers had with prototype development work and their capacity for being able to produce the car in sufficient numbers. Also, Kevin Beattie, who was Jensen's chief engineer and his assistant, Mike Jones, had both worked for Rootes in the past so they knew our team and how we worked.'

Like other manufacturers of relatively low quantity, high performance series production cars, Jensen Motors Ltd found the necessary development on their own models expensive. Unlike many of their contemporaries, who could draw from funds from within the company, Jensen had to rely on accepting sub-contract agreements to finance their own projects. For nearly a decade, they had been heavily committed to the assembly of Austin Healeys (100, 100 Six and 3000). Now, with the prospect of a long-term programme involving Rootes, Jensen's future looked extremely promising. The Alpine V8 project came at a

Kevin Beattie, Jensen's chief engineer (left), and Mike Jones, his assistant. Both had previously worked for Rootes and thus knew how their development team worked. (Photos: Jensen Owners Club).

convenient interval in their working calendar for, while they had work to attend to on their own models, the latter part of 1963 to the beginning of 1964 was not a particularly busy time for them. The Jensen CV8 had been introduced in late 1962 with a Mk II version appearing at the 1963 Motor Show. It was not to be until 1966 that a successor, the Interceptor series, was brought out. This interval between the two models provided Kevin Beattie with the crucial time he needed to work on the Rootes project.

Ian Garrad remained in Britain for over three weeks. During this time he had several meetings with Lord Rootes to discuss the potential market for the new car, and also made several trips up to MIRA with Rootes' development engineers. When he returned to Los Angeles, he left the white Shelby Alpine V8 behind, for this was to form the basis from which Jensen were to work. The original Miles-built red automatic version had remained in America. Now fitted with a manual gearbox, it was used for further development purposes before it was finally disposed of.

At this time, it was Rootes' policy to nominate a project engineer for each of their new designs. The man chosen for the Alpine V8 was the brilliant Alec Caine, who had been apprenticed with Rolls-Royce. Alec was also the project engineer for the Alpine and remembers that he was not particularly impressed by the Shelby prototype: 'When we in the engineering department finally viewed the car, we were not encouraged. It had a most peculiar steering arrangement.' (He was referring to the steering column which was fed through the left-hand inner wing section by means of universal joints, in order to clear the larger engine.) The V8's development engineer was the highly experienced Don Tarbun who, like Alec, knew Kevin Beattie from earlier days. Clearly, it was going to be a formidable team. The experimental department, where the engineers would be working, was situated in the old Humber building which formed part of the Stoke plant. This still retained its old name of Humber Experimental Department, although the entire complex was known as the Rootes Stoke Plant.

Don Tarbun vividly remembers his first encounter with the Shelby prototype. 'This white car arrived and I went out to take it for a test drive. Up until then, I had only driven small-engined cars so I was in for a bit of a shock. I got in, switched on, revved the engine and dropped the clutch. The back axle hopped so much, I thought it would explode. It certainly looked promising.'

Alec Caine, project engineer for both the Alpine and the Tiger (left), and Don Tarbun, the Tiger's development engineer.

News of the proposed V8 Alpine reached the British motoring press in October, one month before negotiations between Ford of America and Rootes were finally completed. In its 'News and Views' column on 25 October 1963, *Autocar* reported: 'A verbal agreement exists between the Rootes Group and Ford International to produce a version of the Alpine with a V8 power unit. American sources state that the 260 cu in is the most likely to be used although a 290 cu in has been tried experimentally. It will drive a Salisbury axle through either a Ford four-speed gearbox or a Ford Cruisomatic three-speed automatic transmission. The price is expected to be about $1,000 more than that of the Alpine in the USA. Once necessary documents have been signed, production is likely to start in December.'

A similar article appeared in the magazine *Motor,* dated 30 October, under the heading of 'Thunderbolt'. 'Negotiations are at present in progress between the Rootes Group and Ford America for the sale of 4.2-litre engines. Initially, the car will be sold in America where it is expected to be competitively priced. The use of the Ford engine has been decided upon to enable the car to be serviced by the Ford dealer network of the US.'

The introduction of the name 'Thunderbolt' caused some confusion, even amongst Rootes themselves. However, an article printed in *Motor* dated 27 November explained the entire matter. Under the heading 'What is a Thunderbolt?' they went on to say, 'In our November 13 issue, we drew attention to the fact that the Sports Car Club of America, in its recently issued classification list of sports cars eligible for the various production categories, included a Ford Thunderbolt in Class B. As this class includes the Aston Martin DB4GT, Ferrari 250GT, and Jaguar E-type (XKE), this new Thunderbolt was obviously assumed to be a high performance car. Now the SCCA has announced that the Thunderbolt is not a Ford but a Sunbeam. Thunderbolt would therefore appear to be the name given to the new Ford-engined V8 Alpine.'

Rootes Motors Inc. were being a little premature in naming the car 'Thunderbolt' (in honour of George Eyston's car which achieved a world land speed record of 312 mph in 1937). However, in order to be able to enter the Alpine V8 in 1964 events, they were required to register the car with the SCCA in late 1963.

Back at Jensen, preparations were being made to build the first prototype which was to be known as Project No. 870. Jensen engineers had already made sketches of the Shelby car, a Series III Alpine had been sent up from Coventry, and the first of the Ford engines had arrived from America. Everything was ready. At planning meetings held at the Jensen factory, Kevin Beattie, Mike Jones, Don Tarbun and Alec Caine discussed the many intricate details involved in the construction of this first Jensen prototype: body modifications, engine mountings, exhaust system and the alteration of the suspension to handle the heavier engine and higher road speeds. It was considered sensible to substitute Jensen manufactured items wherever possible when parts required uprating; ap-

Rootes chose Jensen Motors at West Bromwich for the Tiger programme, as they had the space, the manpower and the experience. (Photo: Birmingham Post and Mail Ltd)

propriate contracts for production items could be drawn up at a later date.

Clearly, there were going to be many problems which would emerge only after Project 870 had been completed, but with as much detail planning done as was considered possible, in September 1963 work began in earnest. From then on, little reference was made to the white Shelby prototype. Eric Neale, Jensen's chief design engineer, explains how they went about it. 'We had no prototype mock-up like those used on the Alpine to work from. The whole job was done on the drawing board. We quite simply introduced the side elevation and plan silhouettes of the Ford engine onto the Alpine envelope and then considered the bulkhead and floorpan modifications. We then produced a profiled wooden model of the new clutch housing-cum-gearbox cover pressing required. From this, our experimental panel beaters produced a one-off. At the same time, our development vehicle builders were producing a three-dimensional template for gas cutting the original Alpine structure in order to remove the unwanted metal. The new cover was then welded into position, new engine mountings fitted, and the Ford V8 unit installed. After all the clearances had been proved, the car was tested. From this point on, it was just a matter of finishing the model for shaw press tools so that production pressings could be made by Boulton and Paul in Wolverhampton.'

On 14 November, Project 870 was put on the road for the first time. Intended as a project analysis vehicle, it highlighted to both the Jensen and the Rootes engineers the problems involved in putting the car into series production.

Eric Neale, Jensen's chief design engineer, and some of his development drawings:

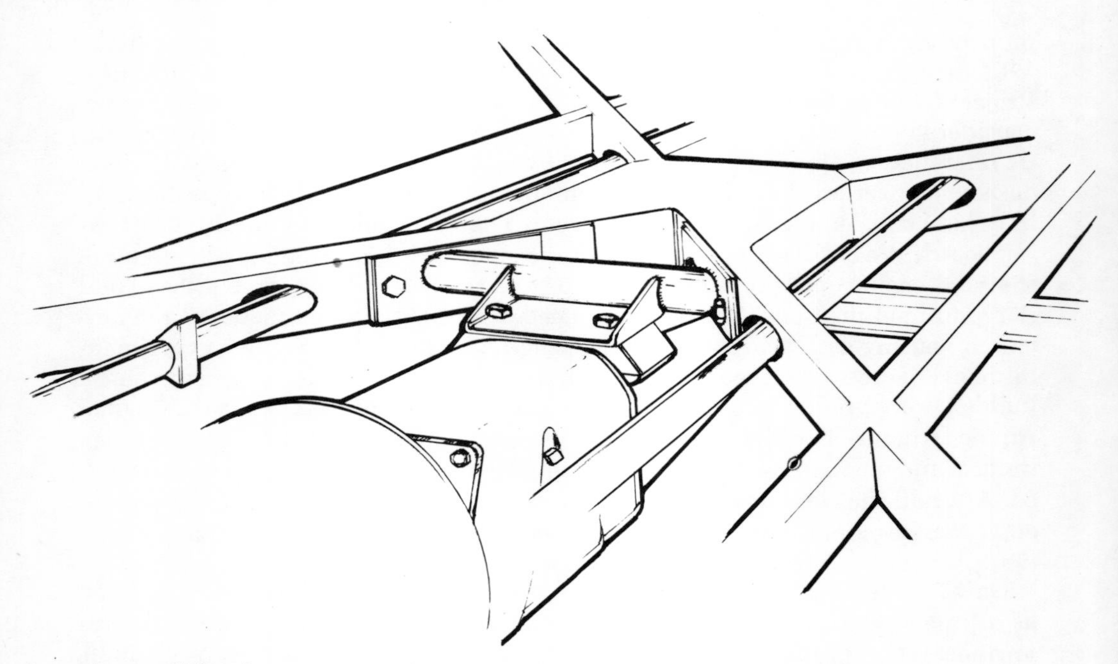

the modifications made to the chassis and rear gearbox mountings . . .

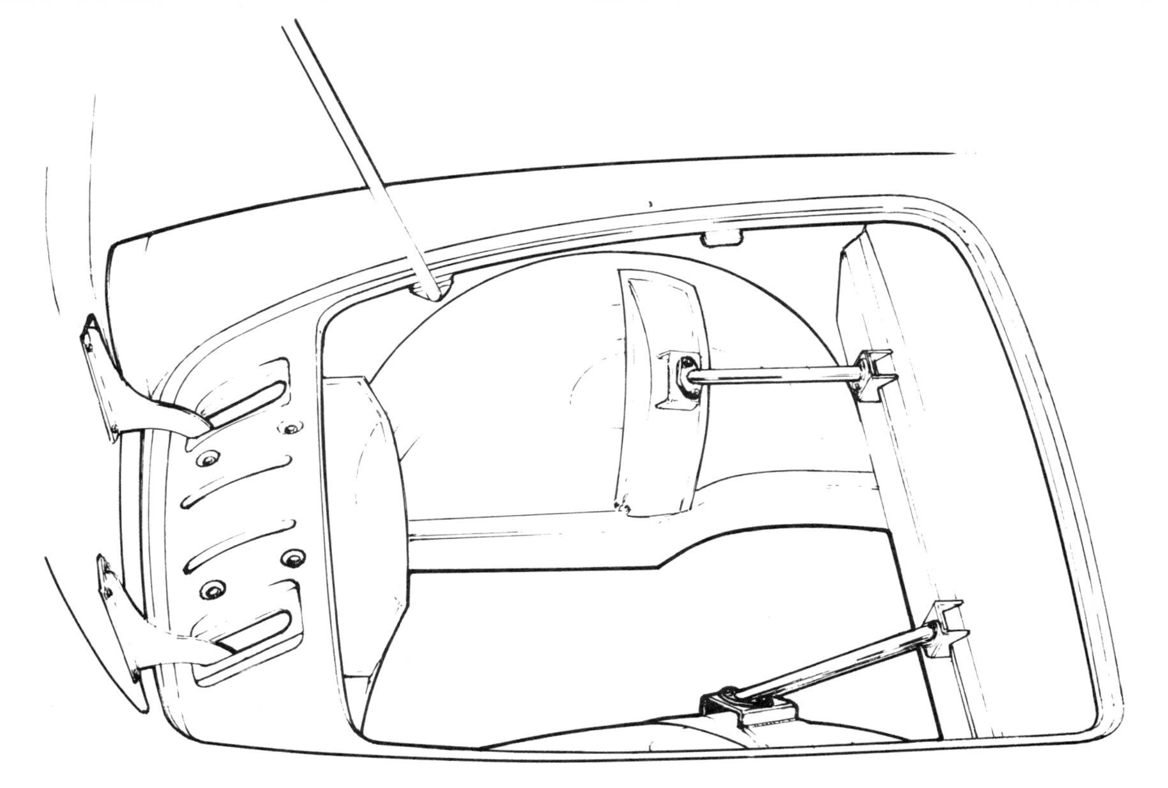

the modification to the engine compartment . . .

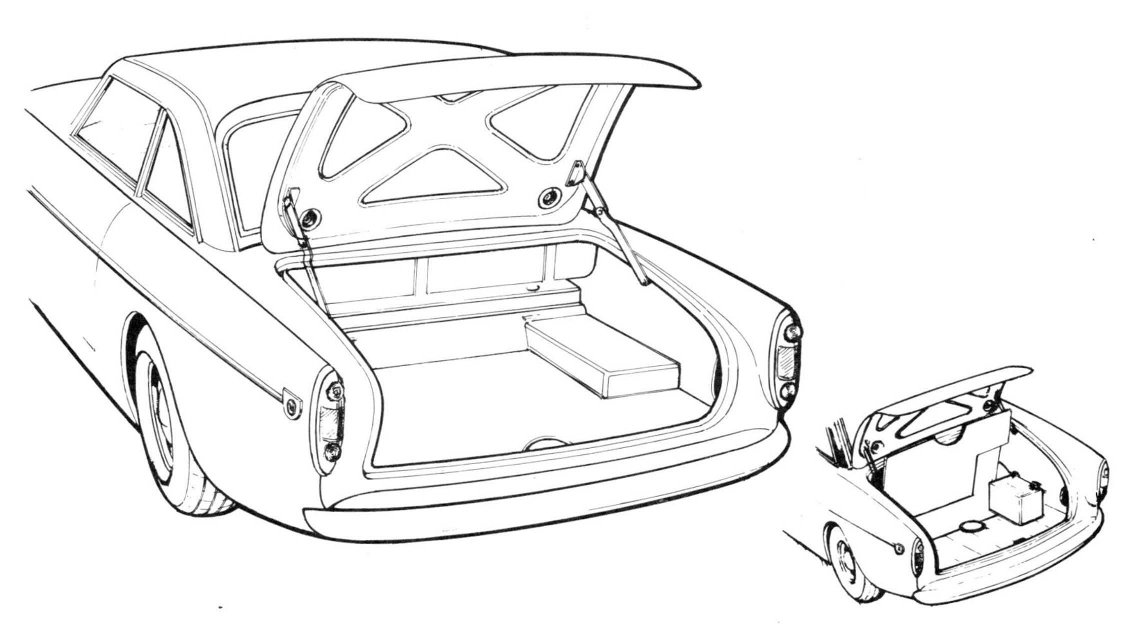

and the modification necessary in order to accommodate the battery in the boot area.

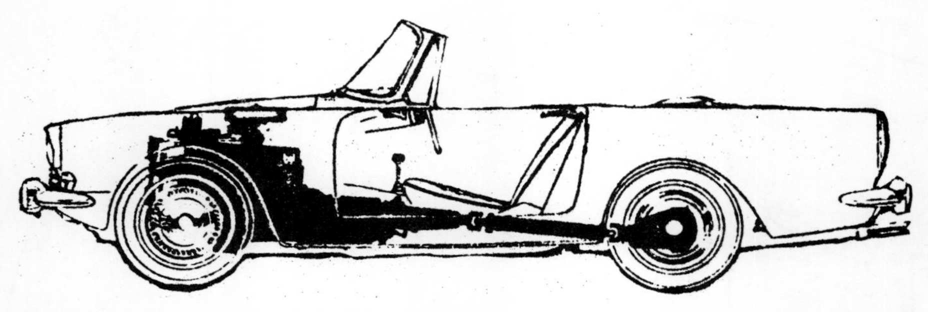

The Tiger in silhouette. By using this technique, Eric Neale was able to determine just how much room was available under the bonnet. Below: *the Tiger in exploded view.*

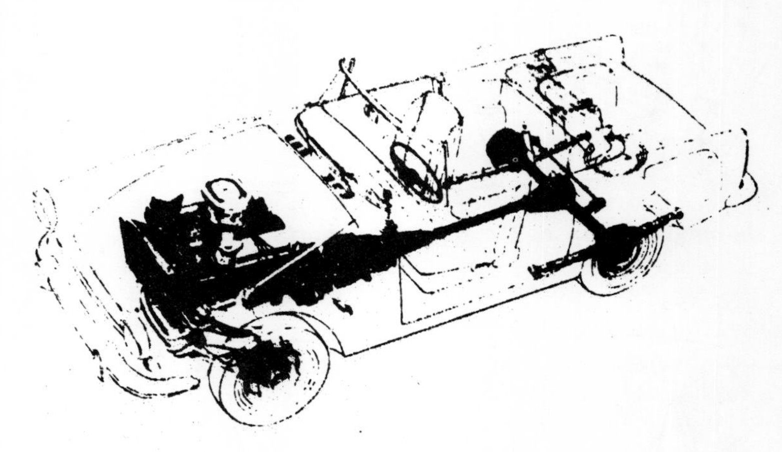

Constructional details such as the new gear box cover were scrutinized for rigidity and the modifications made to the suspension and steering were checked. From these investigations, it was obvious that future cars needed more refinement, and discussions took place in order to outline what was required. For example, Don's first drive in the Shelby car had produced violent axle tramp, which would clearly be unsatisfactory on production cars. Eventually, it was decided that a Panhard rod would reduce the likelihood of tramp under heavy acceleration. Inevitably, this called for a modification to the rear axle in the form of an additional bracket on which to connect the rod and a locating hole in the chassis. The exhaust system, specially developed and built by the Jensen staff, also needed modifying. It consisted of two separate pipes which ran nearly the full length of the car, and was to be rerouted so that it ran through the chassis cross-bracing instead of beneath it. A proper paper element air cleaner for the carburettor was needed, too, and stiffer engine mountings were to be fitted so that the exhaust manifolds did not foul the bodywork on full twist (these stiffer mountings were to cause problems later).

Once the agreement covering the supply of engines had been signed, Leo Lesperance and John Bachman from Ford's commercial sales department, together with John Panks, visited Rootes to arrange the delivery details. Following these discussions, Ford agreed to make certain alterations to the engines. In fact, what was initially thought to be simply a question of packing V8 engines (complete with clutches and gearboxes) into crates and sending them to England, posed several major problems for the men from the giant American motor company. The water pump, crankshaft pulley and generator mounting brackets were all revised, to move them rearward. The mechanical fuel pump was removed and a blanking plate substituted. The oil level dipstick and tube were modified, together with the oil filter, to bring them into a verical position. Finally, specially strong packing cases had to be used in order that the engines (some were to come by air, others by sea) arrived safely.

During Leo's visit, he was able to meet members of the Rootes engineering, parts and service departments, thus setting up a line of communication capable of dealing with any problems which might arise in the future.

But planning the production of the new car formed only a part of the scene, for Rootes also had to determine a comprehensive sales strategy. As early as June 1963, under the instructions of John Panks, Ian Garrad had produced a market evaluation study, so that an estimate of potential sales could be calculated and presented to the Rootes board for consideration. Now that Jensen had been given the Alpine V8 project, these estimated sales figures could be measured against possible production flow. A detailed study revealed that the two figures were very similar, at approximately 290 units per month, and so the obvious decision was taken to export all the initial production to America. However, before production could begin, testing and development work had to be carried out, using over a dozen prototype and pre-production cars.

More and More Tests

By the early 1960s, Rootes had established an enviable reputation in America for producing cars of style and quality. Journalists often used phrases such as 'well appointed interior' and 'considerable attention to detail' when describing a new range. The secret lay in Rootes' competent design studios and the rigorous testing and development programme afforded to each new model. The new Alpine V8 was to be no exception.

The first phase of Rootes' intensive development programme was to be centred on the first Jensen prototype, Project 870. Briefly, this car consisted of:

1. Converted Series III Alpine body
2. Warner T10 gearbox
3. Salisbury 4HA rear axle 3.07:1 ratio
4. 16:1 rack and pinion steering unit
5. Fabricated RH exhaust manifold
6. Fabricated steering arms
7. Prototype radiator
8. Fabricated panels for bulkhead, gearbox cover and wheelarch stiffeners.

In December 1963, Don Tarbun and Alec Caine were able to give the car a short Continental road test when they visited the Touring factory in Milan. The engine had already been run in for 750 miles which included 15 miles of pavé at

MIRA. On 2 December, Alec and Don left Coventry for Maidstone (Kent), where they stayed overnight before flying out to Le Touquet. Then it was on, via Avallon, to Milan, where they were joined by Peter Wilson and Kevin Beattie.

Alec and Don stayed in Milan for two days before leaving for Britain on Saturday, 7 December, arriving back in Coventry on the following Tuesday. The return journey took them via northern Spain (for dust penetration tests) and across France.

They covered a total mileage of 2280 miles and the car averaged 19.1 mpg over a route which was specially chosen to encompass all manner of road conditions, including motorways and Alpine passes. The weather, too, was varied, with rain dominating the drive out and thick snow the return journey.

For most of the trip, the engine behaved well, but there were some minor snags. It showed a tendency to hesitate on pick-up under hard acceleration, and was difficult to start when hot. The engine temperature at sustained high speeds was also considered high. Tests indicated that the cooling system would boil un-

Cutaway drawing of the Ford V8 engine. Its compact design and light weight were the main reasons why this power unit was so suitable for the Tiger. Note the front mounted distributor, another factor in its favour. (Photo: Chrysler UK)

The Ford HEH type gearbox and clutch as used in the Tiger. The transmission is quite strong enough to handle the power from the engine. (Photo: R. May)

der sustained maximum throttle opening at an ambient temperature of 92°F (33.3°C), and thus fell short of Rootes' normal standards (ie that the cooling system be capable of withstanding maximum speed conditions at 104°F/40°C standard and 120°F/49°C heavy duty). Yet the cooling system was considered to be at least comparable with that fitted to the Shelby mock-up, which had successfully withstood high speed runs in the Mojave Desert and the congested traffic of Los Angeles. From this, the development engineers inferred that by installing a Humber-produced radiator of still greater efficiency, the cooling problems would be solved. How wrong they were!

The gearbox synchromesh was thought to be good on all forward gears, although the gear stick was too short and there was some 'chatter' from the lever above 3200 rpm.

Suspension on the test car was entirely satisfactory, apart from a tendency to 'choppiness' from the rear end on certain surfaces. The steering proved to be light, precise and quick. Braking was judged adequate, with particular reference to the relatively undemanding driving conditions prevalent in the States. However, there was fluid vaporization during the Mont Ventoux tests on the return journey. This did not augur well for the twisty, hilly roads of Europe, and gave rise to the suggestion that disc brakes all round would be desirable for the European market, together with larger (14 inch) wheels. Unfortunately, as time was at a premium, this suggestion, along with others concerning the improvement of roadholding, suspension and performance, could not be incorporated into the first production models. But could these ideas form the basis for a Series II model? Incredibly, even before production had begun, the Rootes engineers were thinking already of an improved version.

By the end of January 1964, the Jensen prototype had coverėd nearly 5000 miles. Its original engine had been replaced at 4000 miles, after one of the test drivers had over-revved it. This had caused one of the valves to fail, whereupon the engine stopped! Clearly this must have worried Rootes' development engineers, for they decided that the owners' handbook should warn drivers not to exceed 5000 rpm for continuous high speed motoring. In addition, the possibility of fitting a higher ratio rear axle was considered — possibly of 2.88:1, and further tests were carried out on the cooling system. From these, a temporary specification was drawn up:

1. Jensen-built radiator
2. American-style number plate removed, to reduce airflow restriction to radiator
3. Redesigned fan cowl
4. Cooling system pressurized to 13 psi

Over in Los Angeles, Ian Garrad and John Panks had set about organizing a market research and promotion campaign for the new model. So that they could include details of the car's performance in this advance publicity, the Rootes executives in America asked the development engineers in Coventry to provide them with a full set of figures. So, with its new engine hardly run in, the prototype was taken on a test run. Unfortunately, a flat spot on the initial opening of the throttle caused poor performance in top gear between 10 and 30 mph. Nevertheless, the development team noted with some satisfaction that the prototype had better top gear performance than the Jaguar fixed head E type, and that its 0-60 mph time of 8.65 seconds was bettered only by the Aston Martin DB4, the Jaguar E type, and the Chevrolet Corvette Sting Ray. An experimental memorandum was subsequently written to that effect, and the performance figures forwarded to the United States.

With the first prototype car running satisfactorily, Rootes arranged for Jensen to build more V8 prototypes. Built under the strict supervision of Kevin Beattie, Alec Caine and Don Tarbun, these projects were known as AF1, AF2, etc — AF standing for Alpine Ford. As the first production Alpine V8s were all to be exported to America, these prototype cars were all built in left-hand drive form. By the end of January more Ford engines had arrived from Detroit and more Alpine body/chassis units had been delivered to Jensen. With the exception of AF1 and AF2, these bodies were substantially different to those used on the first prototypes, for by this time Rootes had introduced their MkIV Alpine. These Mk IV pressings featured modified rear wings, the trailing edges being cut off vertically, which resulted in a less dart-like shape when viewed from the side.

By March 1964, the Jensen engineers had built eleven protypes and they were all in various stages of testing. AF1 was to be the Le Mans race test vehicle, and had been sent to Brian Lister's workshop in Cambridge for modification. At the same time AF2 was completing a rough road or pavé test at MIRA, while AF3 had been flown to Carroll Shelby in California for modification in preparation for racing in America.

Endurance testing, a crucial aspect of vehicle development, was undertaken by special drivers from the Car Collection Company, using AF4 and 5. AF6 was still being tested by Jensen's planning department, while AF7 was in the hands of the

One of the development cars under test. The louvres in the bonnet are clearly visible, as is the Alpine badge on the front wing.

The testing area at MIRA. The car in the background is being driven round the banked section used for high speed evaluation.

Humber development department for an extended brake test. It had been suggested that the brake fluid was reaching too high a temperature and that the handbrake was only marginally acceptable. The Humber development engineers considered ways of improving it, but after making exhaustive checks proved that it was the particular handbrake of AF7 which was at fault. The standard handbrake efficiency was judged to be adequate and so no further investigations were carried out.

High speed testing at MIRA formed a critical part of the Tiger test programme. When negotiating the banked section at full throttle, the car was in a constant state of drift and a set of tyres was expected to last no more than three laps! Initially, the road testing was conducted over carefully planned national routes where the cars covered several thousand miles. Misfiring, which had been common to all cars, was traced to faulty plug leads and the offending parts were sent back to Ford (Detroit) for evaluation. High speed cooling tests were also carried out using louvred bonnets but the results showed a reduction of only $3\frac{1}{2}$°C (6°F) — not sufficient, in the opinion of the development engineers, to justify a permanent modification. The rear axle ratio on AF7 had been changed from 3.07 to 2.88 and this had produced a satisfactory 15°C (27°F) drop in engine temperature.

AF8 had been completed by the Jensen engineers and was ready for the showroom, thus gaining the distinction of being the first V8 Alpine car to go on display before the general public. Appropriately, the 1964 New York Motor Show was chosen for the car's debut.

AF9 and 10 were the first two pre-production cars. These models featured all the modifications which had been accepted by the development team to date, together with trim alterations that were to be incorporated on future production models. These modifications included:

larger cross-flow radiator
production rack and pinion steering
fabricated exhaust system
retrimmed interior (to cover new gearbox tunnel)
recalibrated dashboard instruments

At the beginning of March 1963, Jensen Motors were ready to fit the engines into the pre-production cars. In order to gauge how much power these engines would produce, they were taken straight from their packing cases and tested on the bench. The first engine, complete with gearbox and exhaust system, produced 135.5 bhp at 4200 rpm, while the second produced 135.8 bhp at 4200 rpm under similar conditions. The tests also revealed that both units suffered from misfiring above 4000 rpm, which obviously required further investigation. The front mounting rubbers of one of the engines were damaged by heat from the manifolds, indicating that manifold heat deflectors should be fitted to the production cars.

The 4.2 litre V8 engine installed in the Alpine engine compartment. With so little space around the engine, air circulation was poor, causing overheating problems. (Photo: Chrysler UK)

An extract from the first Sunbeam Tiger sales brochure.

One of the five pre-production Mk II Tigers, seen here in San Jose, California. (Photo: R. McLeod)

On 9 March 1964 there was a meeting of the test drivers involved with AF4 and 5 (the two cars used for endurance testing purposes), and a progress report was issued on the basis of their findings. AF4 had completed 15,000 miles fitted with a Ford manual gearbox, while AF5 had completed 13,400 miles with the Borg-Warner gearbox. Both cars had undergone continuous driving over two agreed routes which included both motorway and general purpose roads. Both cars were running with 2.88:1 rear axles and special radiators which had been fabricated by Bowmans. Later, these were replaced by Humber-made units. The overall fuel consumption of AF4 was calculated to be 18.8 mpg while that of AF5 was 20.6 mpg. Both had oil pressures of between 45-50 psi at 2000 rpm.

From the progress report, here is a selection of the faults and the engineers' comments:

Flat spot at 1000 rpm	To be eliminated by Ford (modification to carb)
Third gear position out of reach	Tests to be carried out with cranked lever
Down shifts difficult after cold start	Ford advised
Steering wheel loads excessive at low manoeuvering speeds	Numerically higher ratios to be specified for production
Excessive tyre scrub at large angles of steering lock and car directionally sensitive to road camber changes	Unavoidable due to steering geometry and negative Ackerman geometry
Ankle ache at low throttle openings	Pedal position lowered to that of brake and clutch for production
Weak horn	Tests being carried out with higher volume horns
Noisy fuel pump	Tests being carried out with feed pipes and pump mounted in rubber
Scuttle rattle	Source of rattle under investigation
Excessive wind noise from soft top	As Alpine 1600 soft top — new type under review

Due to the very nature of the Alpine V8, Rootes anticipated from the outset that they would have to make certain unavoidable compromises in certain areas. However, the realized that as the majority of sales would be in the United States, some compromises (for example, the disc/drum brake arrangement) would be quite acceptable. In fact, some of the problems which had been experienced under British test driving conditions would not arise in America at all. In contrast the enthusiastic cornering and braking which is so much a part of the average European sports car driver's technique would almost certainly show up the nose-heavy handling and a braking system liable to fade under heavy use.

Towards the end of March 1964, Peter Wilson sent an internal memo to Peter Ware comparing the relative performance figures of the Austin Healey 3000 and the Alpine V8. It suggested the intended market area of the new car and highlighted the performance differences between the two cars. The memo concluded: 'Studying the performance figures, several points emerge.

'1. The Healey is fitted with overdrive, hence the good top gear performance/acceleration figures as this gear will not allow maximum speed to be reached. The overdrive is only slightly higher in mph per 1000 rpm than the V8 top gear.

'2. The chopped-off-at-the-top power curve of the 260 cu in shows up in acceleration times in the upper speed ranges above 80 mph.

'3. The steady speed fuel consumptions are also affected by this type of power curve. Up to 50 mph we are compatible with the Healey in overdrive, above 70 mph we are comparable with the Healey in direct top and noticeably worse in overdrive.

'Hence the need to consider a higher power version of the Ford V8, the obvious one being the 289 cu in (4.7 litre) "high performance" (hi-po) engine with one 4-choke carburettor which gives 210 bhp at 4400 rpm and 300 lb/ft of torque at 2400 rpm. I am getting an estimate made of the car's performance fitted with this engine. I certainly feel that there will be a demand for increased performance as all the present performance can frequently be used.'

Ford of America offered an impressive range of performance options for the '260' engine but inevitably the benefit of the additional horsepower was only realized at higher engine rpm. Clearly, Wilson was thinking that the increased power of the larger engine would show a benefit all round. But was this extra performance really necessary? Even before the car had been put into production, it was running into conceptual conflict and already there were some in the Rootes engineering department who considered the Alpine V8 underpowered.

By the beginning of April, AF7, which had been fitted with a 2.88:1 rear axle and a Warner gearbox earlier in the year, underwent steady state and average speed fuel consumption tests. These were carried out with an 'after-burner' fitted to the exhaust system, in order to comply with future US emission regulations. This car was later transferred to Rootes' publicity department and used in a photographic session by *Autocar*.

Even at this stage, the car still lacked a name. 'Thunderbolt,' the designation used by the Rootes representatives in America for the SCCA registration, was finally abandoned when it was discovered that the name had already been taken up by another manufacturer. The name 'Sunbeam Tiger' was finally selected in

The idea came from John Panks. 'Let's call it Sunbeam Tiger', he said, in honour of the record-breaking V12. And they did. (Photo: Chrysler UK)

honour of Sir Henry Seagrave's record-breaking V12. The idea came originally from John Panks who, as an early Sunbeam enthusiast, felt that it was aptly suited to the new car. Unfortunately, the name 'Tiger' had already been adopted by Leyland for one of their truck ranges, but this problem was resolved at a meeting held between the chairmen of Rootes and Leyland.

The New York Motor Show was to be held in early April 1964, and Rootes had hurried to complete the Tiger programme so that a car could be exhibited on the Rootes Motors Inc stand. Advanced publicity for the new car had already been issued by the Rootes distributors in the United States; it was therefore imperative that the car arrived in time. AF8 was taken to Ladbroke Hall (Rootes' London-based headquarters) where it was prepared for showroom display before being shipped to America. Following Garrad's return to Los Angeles, the American-based executives had kept in constant touch with the parent company over development proceedings involving the prototype vehicles. But while they may have been privy to all the technical innovations, clearly they were very much in the dark over the car's final appearance. When AF8 arrived, Panks and

The similarity between the Alpine and the prototype Tiger is all too obvious from this angle. To make the New York Show car different, Panks added an egg-crate grille (as used on the first Cobras) and a chrome strip along the body. (Photo: Autocar)

Garrad were very disappointed: they thought that the Tiger lacked style and distinction. How could they justify charging the would-be customer $3500 when the car looked so much like the Alpine? The influence of Lord Rootes was obviously very strong and the result was just what he had envisaged. Only the twin exhaust pipes protruding from beneath the rear valance, and the badges displaying 'Alpine 260' differentiated this pre-production Tiger from the production Alpine. As it happened, at an earlier meeting held in Coventry between the development team and the test drivers, one of the criticisms made of the car was that it looked indistinguishable from its four-cylinder sibling.

Panks realized that the similarity between the Alpine and the Tiger would not escape the attention of the motoring Press and the American public alike. His greatest fear was that the car would be prejudged and then disregarded rather than being considered as something totally new. Clearly, there was little time to make any elaborate alterations, and in any case they would have been circumscribed by strict financial limits. Eventually, just two simple modifications were made to the show car: a horizontal chrome stripe was added at waist height, and the standard Alpine grille was replaced by an 'egg crate' version. These simple trim details must have caught the imagination of the Coventry design studios, for the chrome stripe was later incorporated in the production models. However, it was not until the MkII car appeared that the egg crate grille was added, whereupon the chrome strip was deleted.

The New York Show deadline was met, and there on Stand 12 was what the official catalogue described as the 'Sunbeam Alpine 260'. In the opinion of one American motoring journalist the launch of the new Rootes V8 turned very few heads. He may have been guilty of prejudging the car, but fortunately it seems

The Rootes stand at the 1964 New York Automobile Show. Father and son investigate the Ford V8 as used in the Tiger but their loyalty seems to be placed further afield. (Photo: Autocar)

that the American public were not that easily deceived. The 1964 New York Motor Show was an outstanding financial success for Rootes Motors, with record sales totalling £4½ million, the majority of these orders being for the new Alpine V8. Obviously, the Tiger's similarity to the Alpine was no drawback as far as the American market was concerned. Lord Rootes' vision of the car as a wolf in sheep's clothing had been vindicated — he had been right after all!

That there were so many orders for the new car at the show was all the more remarkable in view of Rootes' misleading publicity. Their advertisement in the official show programme read, 'Have you met our *automatic* Tiger?' (my italics), although only a manual version could be ordered.

Meanwhile, the development work continued. The crankcase ventilation system fitted to the Ford V8 engines received by Rootes up until May 1964 did not meet either the New York or the Californian exhaust emission regulations. This problem was overcome by replacing the old filler cap with a sealed version which featured a flame trap and connecting the oil filler tube to the 'clean' side of the air cleaner. The 'white' Shelby prototype car had now been returned to America where Ian Garrad arranged for a 289 cu in (4.7 litre) engine to be installed. 'We knew that eventually this would replace the 260,' recalls Garrad, 'and we wanted to see how it would perform.' By all accounts, the results were very encouraging.

AF5 in Morocco. The development team hoped the trip might resolve the overheating problems, but unfortunately nothing was proved.

Further testing in progress for one of the prototype cars. Louvred bonnets were never used in production as it was thought that oil vapour might pass through and cover the windscreen.

Despite continued development, which had included revised radiators and different final drive ratios, the development team were still not entirely happy with the cooling. In early May 1964, Don Tarbun took AF5 to Morocco in an attempt to cure the malady. Low ambient temperatures prevented the trip from being a success, none of the tests or modifications proving conclusive. However, Don suspected that the fan was not as efficient as it should be and suggested that electric fans be installed instead. This was investigated but the extra cost involved was not considered to be justifiable.

One problem which proved a little hazardous for the development team in the early days was the Tiger's habit of catching fire! Soon after the initial prototype cars had been built, it was considered necessary to fit stronger engine mountings to prevent the engine from rocking too much. Unfortunately, this also had the effect of causing the Ford carburettor needle to vibrate and eventually to bind, causing petrol to flood the carburettor. A trip to a Ford specialist in South London produced the answer: a three-lobed needle.

By the end of May, most of the testing and development work had been completed. AF2 had been used by the service department for the production of service literature and then returned to the Humber experimental department, where a vertical flow radiator was fitted in place of the existing cross-flow type. This was intended to be a cost-saving measure, but in fact it was proved that the vertical flow type would hardly affect tooling charges and so the idea was dropped.

The Jensen engineers had been using AF4 in conjunction with various testing programmes. These included the design of a gear lever which would make first and third gears easier to reach, and investigation into a steering column rattle which had come to light during the endurance testing. Jensen also investigated the possibility of fitting 14 inch road wheels, but these had yet to be tested on the pavé. After Don's return from Morocco, AF5 was fitted with a production front cross member which incorporated a revised steering rack mounting angle. A new Salisbury rear axle with modified gears had also been fitted which reduced the level of gear whine and, therefore, gave a much quieter ride. Finally, brake evaluation was to be carried out using several different makes of pads and linings to determine the most suitable.

AF7 was being used for steering and suspension tests while AF9 and 10, the two pre-production cars, were in the hands of the car investigation department, Rootes' quality control analysts. AF11, the first right-hand drive vehicle, had been completed and road tests initiated. As soon as the engine had been run-in, it was offered to the management for their comments.

To avoid production delays, contracts had been drawn up with manufacturers such as Lucas and Salisbury for the supply of parts. Items such as speedometer heads and tachometers, steering racks and radiators, differentials and exhaust systems, carburettor air cleaners and chrome trim were all sub-contracted to outside suppliers. Arrangements were also made with Pressed Steel Fisher (who made the Alpine bodyshells) to increase the supply of body units.

Although production was imminent, there was no check to the flow of new ideas from the imaginative Alec Caine. A cold air ventilation scheme for the footwells was on the drawing board, together with a stowable hard top. This was to be collapsible so that it could be fitted in the boot when not in use. Alec's ventilation modification was eventually adopted, but plans to develop the collapsible hard top were cancelled although Jensen did fabricate a prototype.

With a few problems still to be overcome, production of the Tiger was set to commence on 27 June 1964. Arrangements were made for ready 'trimmed' bodies to be transported direct from Pressed Steel Fisher to Jensen Motors. There, the bodies were modified, the engines and transmissions installed and the contracted components, such as Microcell seats, fitted. Rootes realized that while they had to continue with the development programme, it was essential — especially in view of the success of the New York Show — that there should be no production delay. Inevitably, this would mean that the first production cars would have detail differences when compared with later models. For example, the first 56 cars built were fitted with the Borg-Warner T10 gearbox, which un-

Close-up of the short Cobra-style gear stick, which made changes into first and third gear an uncomfortable stretch.

fortunately had rather higher intermediate ratios than the Ford version used subsequently. Also, until the supply of the higher 2.88 final drive became available, the lower 3.07 version was fitted. The short gear shift (similar to the one used in the AC Cobra) still made selecting first and third gears rather difficult, but this was soon overcome when Ford began fitting the lengthened lever. In addition, a small number of early cars were built with PVC facias; later, the wood-veneer type was standardized throughout.

Apart from these initial detail modifications, what were the major differences between the Mk IV Alpine and the production Tiger?

On the production line, alterations had to be made in the engine compartment, to allow for the installation of the Ford V8 engine. One problem was to create enough width to accommodate the two banks of cylinders. A small concave area had to be made in the right-hand inner wing to clear the generator, and the top-hat section inner wheel-arch supports were reduced in height. In addition, extra space had to be found in the bulkhead area as the larger engine protruded further backwards. This was provided by fitting a new clutch and gearbox tunnel which was much lower and wider than on the original Alpine.

It is interesting to note that while the American V8 was somewhat heavier than the British four-cylinder unit, the overall weight distribution remained very similar at 51.7:48.3 front to rear. Fortunately, the very compact design of the Ford engine meant that it was a mere 3.5 inches (88.9mm) longer and only 2 inches (50.8mm) higher than the Alpine's unit. An ingenious modification made by the Jensen engineers was the use of the defunct Burman steering box mountings. Equipped with a set of cast iron brackets, these were used to carry the forward

This is thought to be the only photograph in existence of the Sunbeam Tiger in production. These are left-hand-drive models for export. Note the care taken to avoid damage to the paintwork. (Photo: Birmingham Post and Mail Ltd)

engine mountings for the new power unit. These were of the rubber-in-shear type, as used on all American V8 Fords, the engine being carried on machined surfaces on the underside of each bank of cylinders. In order that the heat from the exhausts did not affect the rubber, small heat deflectors were added on the top of the mountings. A fabricated steel box welded to a cross-member bolted to

Another view of the Jensen factory, in 1966. On the left are Jensen CV8s while on the right is the Austin Healey 3000 production line. (Photo: Birmingham Post and Mail Ltd)

the cruciform chassis carried the rear rubber 'waffle' type gearbox mounting.

All the alterations made to the body/chassis pressings were carried out by the Jensen engineering team, working on the production line.

Surprisingly, the Tiger's brakes were identical to those fitted to the Alpine: 9.85 inch (250.1mm) discs on the front and 9 inch (228.6mm) on the rear, operated by a vacuum servo. Rootes considered them perfectly adequate to handle the extra power.

However, the increase in overall curb weight (2653 lb [1203 kg] for the V8 against 2220 lb [1007 kg] for the Alpine) made it necessary to replace the front and rear springs with stiffer versions. Uprated dampers were substituted and a Panhard rod was added to the rear axle for better location. This had a threaded section which enabled variations in production and wear to be accommodated.

Rootes retained the American Ford electrical ancillaries on the engine, ie the generator, starter motor and coil. However, the voltage regulator and fuel pump were British, manufactured by Lucas and SU respectively.

A much larger crossflow radiator replaced the Alpine's vertical flow type. The Tiger's radiator had its own header tank which was mounted on the left-hand inner wing. To improve the air flow, the valance stiffener beneath the front bumper was cut away, but the starting handle tube was retained to support the rear edge of the panel.

An Engineering Products rack and pinion steering replaced the Alpine recirculatory ball type, and was mounted on the forward side of the front cross member. Owing to the width of the rack, cut-outs had to be made in the front inner wing pressings to allow the steering rack mechanism to pass through. There was little to choose between the steering ratio of the Alpine and the Tiger, the former being 3.3 turns and the latter 3.1 turns, from lock to lock. However, because the Tiger's rack was situated so far forward, the track rods had 'sets' in them, which caused tyre scrub on full lock.

While the Alpine's battery was situated under the front right-hand seat, for weight distribution reasons the Tiger's battery was moved to a specially made

One of the early Tigers, in left-hand-drive tourer form. At this stage, the longer gear stick had yet to be fitted, while the wood veneer dash was intended for the GT only. (Photo: Autocar)

The 'Sunbeam "260" ' displayed on the Rootes stand at the 46th Turin Motor Show, 31 October 1964. The Tiger was first announced on 1 October 1964 for the European market.

well in the boot. The spare wheel was also repositioned, flat on the boot floor, instead of being stored vertically against the rear seat wall.

Initially, Rootes intended to market the Tiger in both GT and tourer form, as with the Alpine. The tourer was to have had a black PVC dashboard, with a hard top available as an extra; while the GT was to have had a veneered dashboard with a hard top as standard equipment. However, Rootes finally decided to drop the tourer in favour of a rationalized GT version.

If a customer ordered a hard top with his Tiger, the car and the hard top were automatically supplied in matching colours. But if the hard top was ordered separately, then it came in black only. With the exception of the courtesy light and sun visor which were fitted to the Alpine GT, the Tiger shared the same luxurious interior as the smaller engined car. An automatic choke on the carburettor explained the absence of a choke control, and the speedometer and rev counter were calibrated in keeping with the different rev range and performance.

By normal standards, the period from conception to production had been very short, and the financial outlay in development had been minimal. The Tiger had got off to a promising start!

Under Scrutiny

It must be with mixed feelings that a manufacturer views the first of a new range of cars as they come off the production line. After many many months of concentrated effort, of living with the project since its inception, ultimately he is in the hands of the buying public. But the buying public is fickle. It can be influenced by advertisements and road tests, and so good publicity is clearly essential. The reactions of the motoring Press to the new Sunbeam Tiger, and in particular their road test reports, make interesting reading.

As early as April 1964, *Autocar* carried a comprehensive article introducing the car to the British public under the heading 'Sunbeam Tiger 260'. Full constructional details together with engineering drawings and photographs of one of the prototype vehicles were included. A cutaway sketch illustrated the installation of the V8 engine.

Not surprisingly, the first complete road test reports of the Tiger were published in the United States. *Road and Track,* for example, posed the question, 'Performance, comfort and reliability at low cost — what more can one ask?' They went on to say, 'In 164 bhp form, the performance and handling of the car are just about ideal for the purpose for which it is intended,' which they considered to be 'as a comfortable and refined sports/touring car.'

Car and Driver in November 1964 declared, 'Tigers are all the rage. Rootes is holding a winner by the tail.' Their background report and road test analysis highlighted the essential differences between the Alpine and the Tiger. They

'This Tiger is mine.' Car and Driver *found the car 'completely transformed' by the installation of the Ford Engine.* (Photo: Stanley Rosenthall)

were honest enough to admit that they had approached the car with considerable scepticism but had found the Sunbeam completely transformed: '. . . the level of the performance is pushed upward to a point that would be impossible with the original engine — no matter how highly tuned it might be.'

Both *Road and Track* and *Car and Driver* agreed that the car needed wider wheels. A 245 bhp version (costing approximately $250 more than the standard car) tested by *Road and Track* showed how the Tiger would perform with additional horsepower. The car had been fitted with Traction Master anti-tramp

Interior of one of the early Tigers sent to America for road testing by the motoring magazines. Note the PVC facia.

bars while the engine had a different camshaft and a four-barrel carburettor.

'A ripsnorting British bomb which can't be beat in its price class,' said McCahill in *Mechanix Illustrated* (December 1964). 'The new Tiger on wheels', he went on, 'is one of the sportiest Gran Turismo buckets to come howling down the pike in many a moon . . . My first stop with the comely little beast was the Daytona Speedway. After ten or fifteen miles of warm-up I belted it wide open and did four laps averaging 121 mph, which is good in any league and should be ample for getting Little Notchead to school on time.'

All the American journalists agreed that the Tiger represented very good value for money. McCahill summed up by saying, 'If you're in the market for a sports or Gran Turismo car in this price range, you can't track anything sportier than the Tiger.' Its price was given by *Road and Track* as $3598.

Sports Car Graphic in November 1964 noted that 'Very few will pull this Tiger's tail!' and went on to describe how the bigger engine resulted in a doubling of torque which '. . . has only made the Sunbeam feel *more* solid than ever.'

The Tiger was intended primarily for the American market. This is a very early example — note the white piping on the seats.

'Rootes is holding a winner by the tail.' Most American journalists were very complimentary about the Tiger.

Jerry Titus, who tested the car, took it to Willow Springs racetrack for high speed cruising analysis. His acceleration time of 0-60 mph in 9 seconds was, he thought, 'impressive enough.' He concluded, 'All in all, the Sunbeam Tiger is amazing value for its price. It's got everything you'd expect from a high-performance GT or sports car costing twice as much.'

Clearly, the American motoring magazines were enthusiastic about the Tiger. It seemed that the performance was sufficient and that the price was right. Rootes had successfully produced a sports car which had speed and handling ideally suited to the American roads. The V8 engine, with its effortless power, returned good economy and reliability coupled with performance. The ride was comfortable and the interior decor tasteful. Surely, Rootes could not fail to sell Tigers in the States?

Although the Tiger was exhibited at the Earls Court Motor Show in October 1964, British customers had to wait until early in March 1965 before the car was available on the home market.

In April 1965, twelve months after their introductory article, *Autocar* issued a full road-test report. It began: 'Well-equipped, easy-going sports car with plenty

Maurice Smith, editorial director of Autocar, *at the wheel of a Tiger. A Tiger enthusiast, Maurice ran two during his time as editor.* (Photo: Michael Cooper)

From this angle, the Tiger looks extremely compact. The Minilite wheels were added after Autocar *bought the car from Rootes.* (Photo: Michael Cooper)

of power and vee-8 smoothness; high gearing gives relaxed cruising at 100 mph, predictable handling, but some steering feed-back and poor turning circles; powerful servo brakes; moderate fuel consumption.

'. . . The idea of "mill switching," as the Americans call it, is not new, but for a large British manufacturer to install a foreign engine from a rival firm in one of their own cars is unprecedented. That the changed car should feel so balanced brings as much credit to the basic Alpine design as to the characteristics of the new engine and the development of its installation.'

Motor, in their May 1965 road test, began: 'Successful marriage of big V8 with comfortable sports tourer. Good flexibility, performance and handling more than compensate for bumpy ride on poor surfaces.' *Motor* went on to explain that the Tiger was not just an Alpine with a larger V8 engine but a new car in its own right, and that Rootes in no way intended that the Tiger should encroach upon the Alpine's market. 'The Tiger,' they said, 'is a sports car of the most masculine kind, not in the strength needed to drive it, but in its character . . . Performance figures are impressive: only just outside the select band who reach 100 mph in under 30 seconds.'

Autocar were equally complimentary in their assessment of the Tiger's performance, saying that it was 'a rapid and exceedingly enjoyable car to drive.'

Motor Sport, whose road test appeared in October 1965, said, 'The Tiger's most impressive feature is its excellent, effortless acceleration, even from very low speeds in top gear.'

Most British magazines sought to probe the ride and handling limits of the Tiger. In so doing, they came face-to-face with its biggest failing. All agreed that on good roads the suspension was firm (if a little lively) and the excellent control never dispelled one's confidence. However, on bad surfaces it was a different story. Apart from the furious kick-back from the front wheels to the steering wheel, the ride became very bumpy. *Motor Sport* explained, '. . . the suspension, being stiff enough to kill all noticeable roll except where direction is changed very suddenly as the car is being furiously accelerated, gives a rough, rattly ride on bad roads.'

Autocar perceptively noted that 'There is a good deal of feed-back to the wheel rim from road irregularities, and one senses that the engineers have had to compromise in designing this new steering.' They also criticized the axle tramp they had experienced with fast acceleration, and suggested that perhaps the fitting of radius arms would overcome the problem. In the view of some of the testers, the Dunlop RS 5 tyres contributed to the car's generally good handling.

Motor *magazine putting a Tiger through its paces. The chrome strip is effective in making the car look longer but, oh, those wheel trims!* (Photo: Motor)

While the acceleration figures varied slightly from road test to road test, all the maximum speed figures were short of the official 120 mph quoted by Rootes themselves in advertisements. 117 mph seemed to be the average figure quoted by most magazines.

Somewhat later (in February 1967 to be precise), *Car* magazine added their belated comments: 'It looks such a wonderful idea on paper — small car, big engine, both well sorted. But the Tiger hasn't been an enormous sales success (says George Bishop) and we think we know why. It's much more of a grand tourer than a sports car, and grand tourers need to be quiet and well-sprung if they're to bring ease to the discriminating on long trips like the one we've just made to Italy.'

The target for George Bishop's criticism was, surprisingly, a 4.2 Mk I Tiger. By the time his story was published in *Car,* Rootes had started production of the Mk II version. Presumably, this was an old demonstration car still in the hands of the public relations department.

Before starting to describe the Tiger in detail, *Car* felt that it was important to assess the true character of the vehicle. 'Considered as the sort of high-performance sports car which its name and specification might suggest, the Tiger doesn't even come to the starting line. Its engine is as big as that of an E-type, yet it is hardly in the same class in the performance and handling stakes.'

They went on to explain that they needed to visit Modena in Italy and approached Rootes, who gave them the Tiger for the journey. On the less than

Without the wire wheels so often featured on the Alpine, the Tiger appeared less sporting and even unpretentious in comparison. (Photo: Motor)

The Tiger received excellent publicity in America, where it represented very good value for money. Playboy's *'Playmate of the Year' was even featured with one.*

brilliant roads of Europe, the Tiger's unsophisticated suspension let it down, as *Car* were quick to notice. 'On even French main roads any speed over about 80 to 90 mph had us bobbing up and down as in one of Mr Issigonis' older rubber-sprung midgets, so that the available maximum of around 115 mph remained just a salesman's ball-point.'

Car's price comparison indicated just where the Tiger stood against its rivals. In 1967, at an all-in price of over £1500 (including safety belts) with some extras added, the Tiger cost £300 less than an E-type Jaguar and £400 *more* than a wire-wheeled MGB GT. (1967 prices for standard models, without extras, were: E-type Jaguar, £2068; MGB GT, £1065; Sunbeam Tiger £1471).

In conclusion, *Car* said, 'As a gentleman's tourer the main thing against the Tiger is its price, and the noise and discomfort which discourage its use in the way for which it is presumably intended.'

Perhaps the Tiger's biggest accolade in motoring Press circles was the decision by the editors of both *Autocar* (Maurice Smith) and *Autosport* (Gregor Grant) to

A GREAT NEW ADDITION TO THE SUNBEAM SPORTS RANGE

THE TIGER

V8 4·2 litre engine 0-60 m.p.h. in 9·2 secs top speed over 120 m.p.h.

You expect excitement in a Sunbeam – but never before have discerning drivers experienced anything so exhilarating as the Sunbeam Tiger. 164 bhp take the Tiger from 0.60 mph in 9.2 seconds, and it tops 120 mph. But it's at the other end of the speedo that the Tiger is really amazing – here you have low-speed docility with power in reserve to accelerate away in top gear from 20 mph. With firm suspension, remarkable economy, rack-and-pinion steering, servo-assisted brakes with front discs, fully adjustable seats, walnut facia and instrumentation, the Tiger is the supreme sports car for rallying, motorway or town traffic. ***£1,445.10.5** inc £250.10.5 pt.

SUNBEAM RAPIER

All-synchromesh gearbox gives silken smoothness to the famous Rapier thrust. With it comes firm front suspension for absolute tyre-to-tarmac road-holding; ideal driving position; light, self-adjusting clutch; servo-assisted brakes with discs in front – and 1.6 litre engine to speed you along in the lap of luxury. ***£889.13.9** inc £154.13.9 pt. Overdrive and whitewall tyres as optional extras.

SUNBEAM ALPINE

Sports performance with touring luxury, that's the Alpine. Lively 1.6 litre engine, all-synchromesh gearbox, compound carburettor, swift acceleration to 100 mph with servo-assisted brakes and front discs. Fully adjustable rally-type seats, adjustable steering wheel and control pedals, racing-style gearbox.
Sports tourer ***£853.8.9** inc £148.8.9 pt.
Hardtop available. Gran Turismo Hardtop (with many additional refinements) ***£913.17.1** inc £158.17.1 pt.
Optional extras include Borg-Warner fully-automatic transmission or Laycock de Normanville overdrive on top and third gears, wire wheels and whitewall tyres.

***all prices ex-works**

BY APPOINTMENT TO HER MAJESTY THE QUEEN MOTOR VEHICLE MANUFACTURERS ROOTES MOTORS LIMITED

ROOTES MOTORS LIMITED

LONDON SHOWROOMS AND EXPORT DIVISION
ROOTES LIMITED DEVONSHIRE HOUSE PICCADILLY LONDON W1

SUNBEAM TIGER·ALPINE·RAPIER

Advertisement from Autocar, *25 June, 1965.*

It is very easy to be dramatic when driving the Tiger — even when you have no such intention. This car was also featured in the Autocar *article, 'Under-rated Tiger'.* (Photo: Michael Cooper)

buy Tigers for their own personal use. Both ran a Mk I and later a Mk II.

In his article '10,000 Miles in a Tiger,' Gregor Grant said that the 10,000 miles had been as trouble-free as anyone could wish. He went on to comment that the finish, on the whole, had been 'admirable'; the paintwork, 'first-rate'; the gearbox, 'a sheer delight to use'; and the lighting equipment, 'better than average'. Gregor obviously felt that the car represented good value for he wrote that the price was 'not a great deal to pay for such a splendid motor-car.'

Maurice Smith was equally complimentary, calling his 20,000 mile assessment 'Under-Rated Tiger.' 'It is,' he said, 'one of the most effortless and straightforward cars you can have.'

World's fastest sports car priced under $3600.†

With a gung-ho V-8 and a sure-footed British chassis, Chrysler's Sunbeam Tiger puts high-priced competitors on their very best behavior.

Go ahead. Search under $3600 for a genuine sports car that (1) has 125 m.p.h. capability, (2) does 0 to 60 in 9.2 seconds, (3) turns 100 m.p.h. @ 3900 r.p.m.

There's one—Chrysler's Sunbeam Tiger V-8. And it puts you wheel-to-wheel with the $5500-$7000 jobs.

Tiger's secret? Sunbeam started with a very tough Class F Alpine, built to sell in volume. (100 m.p.h. capability, yet priced under $2500† in the U.S.!) They gave it a potent V-8 power train and modifications to accommodate same, and out came Tiger's unique performance/price proposition.

Spectacular specs

Tiger's own four-speed gearbox is close ratioed, starting with 2.32:1 in 1st. With a 2.88 axle and quick clutch, things happen in a hurry here.

That includes braking. Girling discs (9.85") up front, 9" drums behind. They're self-adjusting at all four corners—and power assisted besides!

It also includes steering. Rack & pinion, 3.1 turns lock-to-lock. Very positive.

On the road, Tiger reacts without surprises in an ess-curve or a drift, and is surprisingly smooth over both bad roads and tar strips.

Comfortable cockpit

With this much punch at the price, you might suspect some short-changing inside. Not so.

We start with handsomely pleated, foam-padded bucket seats. Then make them fully adjustable—with reclining backs.

Then we give you a telescoping steering wheel. Adjustable foot pedals. And footwell ventilation to take the curse off a hot day.

You also get a two-speed heater (standard) for cold days. Plus niceties like a lockable console. A walnut dash. An easy-to-work top. And a big trunk.

Take on a Tiger V-8 at your nearby Sunbeam dealer's. You'll love it—and its $2000 head start on competition.

†Based on mfr's suggested retail prices, East Coast P.O.E., state and local taxes, destination charges and options extra, including outside mirror. West Coast slightly higher.

ROOTES
CHRYSLER'S SUNBEAM

Advertisement for the Tiger as used in American motoring magazines.

In his resumé of the maintenance over the second 10,000 mile period, Maurice emphasized that the Tiger was so reliable that, apart from the usual routine servicing, it required no attention at all. He concluded his assessment thus: 'The Tiger is judged by many, but known by few. Satisfactory and satisfying, it could prove itself to be the answer to many a keen driver's prayer. I am having another one.' And he did.

On 4 March 1965 the Sunbeam Tiger clawed its way onto the British market. At the same time, advertisements appeared in the following newspapers and journals: *Daily Express, Daily Mail, Sporting Life, Autocar, Autosport, Motor, Cars Illustrated, Motor Racing, Motor Sport, Sportscar* and *Sporting Motorist.*

One of the advertisements illustrated the car at high speed, with the headline: 'Sunbeam unleash the Tiger.' Performance figures were quoted as being 0-60 mph in 9.2 seconds with a top speed of over 120 mph.

Typical reactions from the Press included:

> 'From a standing start, the car is cruising at 100 mph in less than half a minute.' — *Daily Telegraph.* (This claim is interesting. Most American road test reports quoted a 0-100 mph time of around 22 seconds, whereas both *Motor* and *Autocar* quoted approximately 31 seconds).
>
> 'I found the Tiger surprisingly docile.' — *Evening News.*
>
> 'In top ratio, the car could be nursed down to almost 10 mph for town work as well.' — *Evening Standard.*
>
> 'As with all Rootes cars, the interior finish is good.' — *Daily Mirror.*
>
> 'Sensible in size, pleasant in appearance, it has delightful road manners and superb performance. To those who have not enjoyed the powerful woofle of a big V8 under the bonnet, the Tiger awaits at a not out-of-the-way price.' — *Sporting Motorist.*

Basil Cardew of the *Daily Express* came straight to the point by stating that 'This is no paper Tiger.' His verdict: '. . . A first-class British-US effort. It is a bit pricey — but what a lot of fun it can give.' The *Daily Telegraph* also featured an article on the car, and their car test driver remarked that he 'did like the remarkable feeling of sail-planing on the motorways.'

The advertisements which appeared in the American Press presented the car as outstanding value for money: 'World's fastest sports car priced under $3600 . . . With a gung-ho V8 and a sure-footed British chassis, Chrysler's Sunbeam Tiger puts high-priced competitors on their very best behaviour.' The copy then stressed (under headings like 'Spectacular specs' and 'Comfortable cockpit') just how much the prospective buyer got for his money.

Rootes' public relations departments on both sides of the Atlantic were not slow in seizing opportunities for displaying the car. In America, a pink Tiger was featured with the 1965 'Playmate of the Year' in *Playboy* magazine.

A Sunbeam Tiger taking part in the Lord Mayor's Show in 1964. It was fitted with electric fans to stop it overheating. (Photo Chrysler UK)

In England, a Tiger (fitted with electric fans to stop the engine from overheating due to the slow speed of the procession) was one of a group of sports cars which took part in the 1964 Lord Mayor's Show.

This, then, was the publicity which surrounded the Tiger. The road test reports were generally encouraging, even enthusiastic, and Rootes had cause to be optimistic. The launch of the car did not, of course, spell the end of the development engineers' involvement, either at Rootes or at Jensen. With production started, there were still modifications to be made and a future development scheme to organize. And the Rootes competition team were about to enter two cars in the Le Mans 24 hours. The Tiger was rising onto its feet and preparing to leap.

Development and Improvement

From the beginning of July 1964, the Tiger development programme assumed a dual role. As the car began to become available throughout America, dealers were able to assess their customers' impressions, and feed the information back to Coventry. Armed with this useful knowledge, the prototype cars were further modified and tested. Allied to this work, was the research necessary for the development of a Mk 11 Tiger, a project which the Rootes management now had firmly in mind. Indeed, it could be said that from mid-1964, all development work was undertaken in order to produce the second generation of Tigers.

In May, AF2 had been fitted with a vertical (as opposed to cross) flow radiator, as a cost comparison exercise, and two months later the car was still undergoing tests in heavy town traffic and high-speed cruising on motorways. The development team considered that the cooling system could be further improved and decided to fit a larger bottom tank to the replacement radiator. However, in Don's opinion, the efficiency of the radiator air intake was still in question. He was convinced that the engine temperature could be reduced if only they could increase the airflow. With this in mind, he drove AF2 up to MIRA for tests, but to no avail. It seemed that the root of the problem was the lack of airflow beneath the bonnet, to which there was no easy solution.

AF5 was being used for brake testing, which involved comparing the relative performance of several different makes of brake pad. Although there was insufficient proof of pad life, results showed that the best braking performance was achieved with a configuration of M59 pads on the front and DON 24 shoes on the rear, together with high boiling point fluid, $\frac{7}{8}$ inch diameter rear wheel cylinders, and the removal of the dirt shields from the front discs. These modifications were then made to the braking system of AF2.

AF6 had been used by the Jensen planning department for construction evaluation purposes and was then handed back to Jensen Engineering for rebuilding, using the specification laid down for the first fifty production vehicles. When rebuilt, it was to be held at Jensen Motors and used as a reference vehicle for investigation purposes, should any problems occur during the early days of production.

AF7 was being used to develop the steering mechanism. Initial tests showed that the steering geometry improved with a set of revised steering arms. However, since there was a delay in the delivery of these replacement arms, the car was moved on to suspension development work, where various configurations of springs and anti-roll bars were tried out.

It was now six months since the first continental trip undertaken by Don and Alec in the prototype car. Lord Rootes wanted to use a Tiger on his holiday in the south of France, and Peter Wilson decided to take advantage of this. He delivered AF7 to Nice and later brought the car back via southern Italy. This enabled him to get a very good assessment of the car over 3500 miles of varied motoring, while enjoying some excellent weather!

Almost since the Tiger project began, the gear noise from the differential had provoked bitter complaints. AF9 was now loaned to Salisbury Transmissions in a bid to find some method of mitigating it.

By the end of July 1964, AF11, the first right-hand drive prototype vehicle, was in the hands of Jensen Motors, who were using it for the following development work:

1. Evaluating a redesigned gear lever with a longer stem (plans of which had been sent to Ford America for them to manufacture it).
2. Designing a larger ash tray.
3. Developing a foot-operated dipper switch that had to be sunk into the gearbox housing.
4. Revising footwell ventilation to overcome the effect of heat penetrating the scuttle.
5. Lowering the clutch pedal position by $\frac{5}{8}$ inch.
6. Modifying the hooter specification using Lucas horns.
7. Testing the car over pavé when fitted with 14 inch wheels and 5.90 x 14 RS 5 tyres.

Two further prototype cars were now under construction. AF12 was to be the second right-hand drive prototype, and also incorporated a rear disc brake

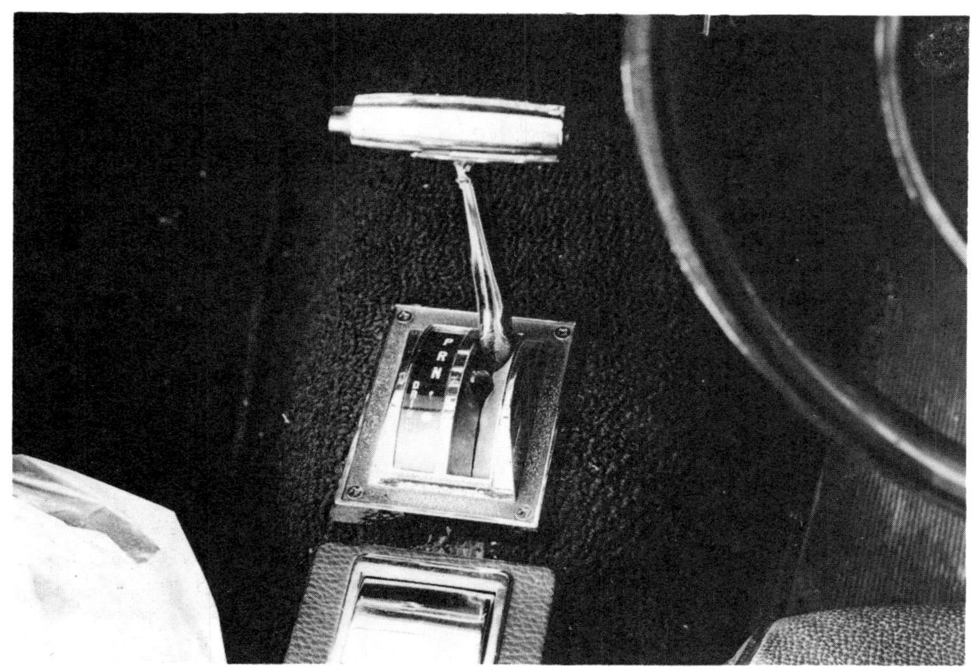

The automatic gear shift fitted to one of the two automatic development Tigers. Neither proved satisfactory.

assembly using Girling components, while AF14 was being built as a Mk 1 automatic.

During 1964, Rootes made a general assessment of the Tiger project. Its development to date, together with a continual demand for improvements for the US market, seemed to substantiate earlier ideas for an uprated version — a Mk II, in fact. Fate was about to play into the hands of those who had always considered the Tiger underpowered, and in this instance, fate came in the form of Ford, Detroit. For they had by now ceased production of the 260 cu in engine, preferring to concentrate on the larger, more powerful 289 cu in unit. Although a supply back-log of the smaller engines would ensure continued production for another 18 months or so, a changeover was inevitable. And so Rootes purchased a small quantity of 289 cu in (4.7 litre) engines for experimental purposes.

During June, AF4 had been involved in an accident. As it had to be rebuilt anyway, Rootes decided to equip this car with one of the larger engines, and at the same time to alter the body trim to that of the proposed Mk II model. Fitted with 14 inch wheels, the rebuilt AF4 was taken to MIRA for performance tests. The results were encouraging, demonstrating that while acceleration was improved, fuel consumption was surprisingly hardly affected.

Although an automatic version of the Tiger had been mentioned when the car made its debut at the New York Motor Show, so far none was available. Nevertheless, Rootes were still thinking of introducing an automatic version as they thought it would be particularly suitable for the two-pedal American market. To enable the Development Team to evaluate how a Tiger would perform with an automatic transmission, AF14, which had already been fitted with a '260' engine complete with a Ford three-speed automatic gearbox, was taken to MIRA. Unfortunately, the results proved that not only was its top speed inferior to that of the manual car but its petrol consumption was markedly worse. The automatic Tiger programme was then temporarily dropped, in the hope that the

One of the prototype cars on the banked circuit at MIRA. The Tiger's maximum speed was always a sensitive issue: whereas the Rootes' development team regularly exceeded 120 mph, road test magazines quoted a top speed of only 117 mph. (Photo: Chrysler UK)

larger '289' engine would produce more favourable results at some later date.

Liaison between Rootes Motors Inc in the States and the engineers in Coventry continued. As supplies of the Tiger began to filter through to the American dealers, it became clear that more modifications were required. Early owners complained of after-boil (when the water in the radiator boils after the engine has been switched off). This had been a problem with early Alpines fitted with cross-flow radiators, but a change to vertical-flow radiators on later cars had cured the trouble. The Tiger had a cross-flow type so, clearly, more investigation was needed. In order to gain experience of the problem at first hand, it was decided that Alec Caine should go to the States.

Once in California Alec made several tests, including driving the car in heavy Los Angeles traffic. On his return to Coventry, one of the suggestions he made was that the radiator core be made of thicker material, to ensure that the water would boil at a higher temperature, while the thicker core would give better heat dissipation after the engine had been stopped.

Throughout the Tiger's development, the Rootes team were particularly conscious of the critical rev limit of the 260 cu in engine, as they feared that this would prove to be a weakness once production had started. 'We had to go to 5000 rpm to get a top speed performance,' recalled Don Tarbun, 'but at 5250, as we knew from bitter experience, the engine exploded. The 2.88 axle was the highest ratio we could get, so we were stuck with it.' In fact, during development, one engine blew up when it was revved to over 5000 rpm (the offending unit was then sent back to Ford in Detroit for a refund!). Although the Rootes engineers regularly achieved a top speed of 125 mph, the motoring magazines' road tests quoted a top speed of only 117 mph. Even Tiger advertisements claimed 'a top speed of over 120 mph' — a discrepancy which could not have gone unnoticed.

In January 1965, possibly the most significant modification of the entire Tiger programme was set in motion.

As a forward development exercise, Jensen Motors were commissioned to convert an existing Sunbeam Tiger to a De Dion rear suspension layout. The car they chose for the work was AF4. It was to be fitted with:

Salisbury 4 HU final drive unit
Dunlop inboard disc brakes of $10\frac{3}{4}$ inch diameter
BRD sliding spline drive shafts
Jensen-designed De Dion tube and hub assembly
Armstrong adjustable dampers
14 inch 5K wheels
590 x 14 Dunlop RS5 tyres

The modified car was taken to MIRA for testing and evaluation so that the new suspension layout could be compared with the standard live axle arrangement.

From the experimental road test report, outlining the results of the MIRA test, the following points emerged. From standing starts, the adhesion using first gear was greatly improved. Further, it was found that it was impossible to spin the wheels on acceleration tests, which indicated that the suspension could handle greater power had it been available. Under power, the car accelerated in a straight line — unlike the live sprung car which tended to lift its offside wheel. The handling was the same on left-hand and right-hand bends, and showed a marked improvement over uneven-surfaced corners where the limit of the cornering speed was dependent on the adhesion of the front wheels — again unlike the live axle arrangement, where the rear end adhesion was lost first.

However, while the test did indicate the advantages of such a suspension layout, there were problems. The rear brakes were too powerful and resulted in instability when braking at high speed. Engine and gearbox vibrations were transmitted to the interior of the car and, while this was only noticeable at low engine and road speeds, it was considered objectionable. Also, the De Dion arrangement had insufficient elasticity which resulted in lumpy gear-changes and exaggerated the backlash of the final drive gears between drive and overrun.

Several suggestions were made. These included the substitution of Girling rear disc brakes, which would be more in tune with the power of the front discs, together with an investigation into the location of the De Dion tube with a view to improving high speed handling.

Clearly, had this type of suspension unit been developed to the point where it could have been incorporated into the production car, it would have eliminated most of the Tiger's handling difficulties. As it was, Rootes considered this a forward development exercise only. They did not feel at this time that the considerable cost necessary to perfect the modification was justifiable.

Meanwhile, Sunbeam Tigers were beginning to appear in American automobile showrooms in increasing numbers. Although both Panks and Garrad had good reason to be pleased, Panks considered that certain details required attention, and contacted Coventry asking for their assistance. For example he thought that the Dunlop RS5 tyres should be replaced by a radial-ply version. As a result, Rootes tested several different makes before finally deciding on Michelin which they made available as an extra. Panks also asked the factory if they could make the exhaust sound more 'sporty' as some American drivers had criticized the 'tame' sound of the Tiger. In response, the development team increased the bore size of the silencer tail pipe to produce the required sound.

Panks remembers that he did have some difficulty in communicating his requirements to Ryton: 'At the time, the company had a fairly ambitious programme of new cars and I was not at the top of the list. Luckily, Rootes had

The 4.7 litre (289 cu in) Ford engine installed in one of the prototype cars. Its external dimensions were the same as those of the smaller unit it replaced. Note the alternator.

one of the most competent engineering teams in the car business. Nevertheless, their main commitment was the development of the Hillman Imp and the forthcoming Hunter (Arrow) range. The sort of modifications I was asking for took time, and it just happened at the wrong period. Initially, Rootes were quite happy to listen but as soon as Chrysler intervened, they wanted to talk Hunters and Imps, not Tigers and Alpines.'

Of course, with Rootes' engineers heavily involved in several new models, it was quite reasonable that Panks's requests were not given immediate priority. Moreover, development of the Tiger was still continuing: by 1965, the Mk II programme was well under way, involving seven cars in all — AF201 to AF207. As many of the early Mk I prototype cars were still running, they continued to be used for development purposes, while the later AF200 series was used for project analysis. AF201, fitted with a '260' engine and featuring all the body refinements of the Mk II, was put on the road in March 1965 to begin testing.

In April 1965 Jensen Motors were commissioned to assemble a prototype Mk

Rear of AF202. This was the second of Rootes' prototype automatic Tigers. It was taken over by Geoffrey Rootes, who used it for some time.

II car equipped with a 289 cu in engine coupled to an automatic transmission, the code name being AF202. By mid-May, the engine had been run in and a preliminary set of performance figures taken. Alas, as with the smaller engined car, both the performance and the petrol consumption were inferior to the manual version. Following this, the idea of producing an automatic Tiger was dropped and no further tests were made. No doubt the poor sales figures for the automatic Alpine in the States were partly responsible, but the deterioration in performance and the increase in petrol consumption (which would have resulted in bad publicity) were also significant factors. Later Geoffrey Rootes took over AF202 as his own personal vehicle, using it continuously for several years.

A report written in May 1965 highlighted the main problems being experienced with the all-disc brake set-up on AF11, 202 and 203. These were excessive handbrake travel after moderate mileage, brake pad rattle when the brakes were off, and rattle from the rear handbrake caliper linkage. All these details were investigated in conjunction with engineers from Girling.

By mid-July 1965 plans were well in hand to introduce a Mk II Tiger. Meetings between the Jensen and Rootes teams discussed the viability in real terms of the updated model, together with the type of detail improvements which were to be made. John Panks, with his intimate knowledge of the American market, was anxious that the Mk II car should be as different from the Alpine as possible yet still remain competitive on price. He well remembered his disappointment over the New York Show car in April 1964 and the trouble he had gone to in adding the extra body trim just to make the Tiger look a little different from the Alpine on display.

As a result of these meetings, a project intention schedule was drawn up outlining the format of the proposed Mk II. In addition to trim alterations and the inclusion of the 289 cu in (4.7 litre) engine and gearbox, it was intended that the brakes be uprated by fitting discs all round and the wheels be increased to 14 inch. Once the schedule was completed, Rootes undertook a production cost analysis and forwarded the results to the States.

When the American dealers were told of the proposed price of the Mk II they were not impressed. 'How can we justify the price increase,' they asked, 'when the car still looks so much like the Alpine?' Indeed, this was a valid argument, for while the Tiger was gaining popularity in the States, its main attraction was undoubtedly its competitive price.

Although this reaction was inevitable, it still came as a bitter blow to the Coventry factory. It was now a case of back to the drawing board. The larger engines had already been ordered from Ford and the body modifications arranged with Pressed Steel Fisher and Jensen. The only option was to cancel the costly rear brake layout for the American Tiger. Adopting the attitude that compromise is no disgrace, a new project intention paper was then drawn up:

Ford 289 cu in (4.7 litre) engine fitted with stronger valve springs and threaded rocker arms giving safe engine speeds up to 5500 rpm.
Ford manual HEH-B gearbox with wide ratios.
Brakes to remain as Tiger I.
Wheels to remain as Tiger I, but painted silver.
Tyres: 5.90 x 13 Goodyear Motorway Speed Specials.
Exhaust system to remain as Tiger I.
Petrol pump: to be repositioned in the redundant Alpine spare wheel well.
Engine oil cooler: required as standard fitting.
New wheelarch and sill mouldings to be introduced.
4 inch wide adhesive tapes (four to each side of the vehicle) to be applied.
'Egg box' grille and surround to replace Tiger I grille.
Removal of chrome strip from side of car.

On 9 August 1965 Rootes introduced their computerized chassis numbering scheme and, accordingly, the code of the Tiger was changed from B947xxxx to B382xxxxxx. This did not signify a model change. All vehicles continued in production as before but were now known as Tiger Mk Ia's.

The 1966 New York Motor Show. The Rootes Motors Inc stand complete with Sunbeam Tiger and 'Tiger' girl. (Photo: Autocar)

In October of the same year a Mk I Sunbeam Tiger was exhibited on the Rootes stand at the Earls Court Motor Show. With the exception of detail alterations which were also featured on the Alpine (footwell ventilators, vinyl bag for the hood, etc.) the car remained the same. Consequently, the publicity was equally uninspiring and reports noted that the marque 'continued as before'.

Rootes had decided to equip the Tiger with an alternator when the 289 cu in engine was introduced. In early October, one was sent over from Ford, Detroit and fitted to AF204. However, the midification proved disappointing, as the alternator fan was found to be very noisy. However, as this car had also been fitted with three-pot disc brakes and 14 inch wheels, as part of the continual development of the Tiger's braking system, testing continued.

When Peter Ware, Rootes' engineering director, requested the use of a Sunbeam Tiger, AF15 (reg. no. EHP 51C) was considered to be the most suitable. It was restored to 'as new' condition, having had a hard life as a development vehicle, and then put at his disposal.

For the past six months, AF6 had remained in the hands of Jensen Motors as a fault-finding reference vehicle, should there have been any snag during the early days of production. As no major problems had come to light so far, it was now released for further development work and in January 1966 it was fitted with a bench-tested 289 cu in engine. Before installation, the engine, complete with air cleaner, fan and test-bed exhaust system, had produced a peak power output of 172 bhp (nett) at 4000 rpm. AF6 was then tested at MIRA and a set of performance figures were taken in order to assess the relative acceleration times with 13 inch and 14 inch wheels. The results revealed that there was an improvement in acceleration over the Mk I car, even with the larger wheels fitted. The car returned almost identical petrol consumption (22.5 mpg) and although high winds made the test track unsuitable for maximum speed runs, it became clear that with the extra power available, top speed would undoubtedly be increased.

By the beginning of February, Rootes and Jensen were ready to embark on the Mk II programme. Jensen were then commissioned to build five pre-production cars to the new specification (using Mk I cars as a basis) and, on 9 February 1966, the first car was assembled using the chassis coding B382001322. The four other cars that followed were:

B382001394 built 23.2.66.
1527 built 28.2.66.
1528 built 1.3.66.
1533 built 2.3.66.

All five cars were fitted with 289 cu in (4.7 litre) power units and HEH-B gearboxes. The engines had alternators in place of dynamos but none of the cars had oil coolers. All five carried the body trim of the Mk II which comprised

The second pre-production Mk II Tiger. This resembled the intended production models for the European market.

The pre-production Mk II Tiger developed for the British market, featuring 14 inch wheels and disc brakes all round. The Minilite wheels were fitted by Autocar *after they bought the car in 1967.*

Had the Mk II Tiger featured all the refinements Rootes originally intended, its retail price would have been close to that of the Jaguar E-type. This was just not viable, and so the plans for larger wheels and disc brakes were cancelled. (Photo: Chrysler UK)

wheelarch and sill mouldings but no waist-level chrome strip and all but the first had egg-box grilles. The first car was left-hand drive and built to the revised North American specification: 13 inch wheels, disc/drum brakes and black and white stripes which were to be a novelty for the States only. The second car was also left-hand drive and featured a similar specification but with no stripes. This was to illustrate the European Mk II Tiger. The third, fourth and fifth cars were all built to the British specification with 14 inch wheels and 10.7 inch disc brakes on the front coupled to 9.7 inch disc brakes on the rear.

With the pre-production cars built and running, Rootes calculated the cost of fitting the Tiger with four wheel disc brakes. Unfortunately, the results indicated that the UK retail list price would be at least £1650, £200 more than the Mk I. In fact, the figures indicated that it would retail at only £300 less than the price of the then current E-type Jaguar coupé (£1934), a car that even Rootes had to agree offered a great deal more performance for the money. From then on it was agreed to standardize to the North American/European specification throughout.

Discussions with John Panks and Ian Garrad over the predicted sales figures for the new car seemed to indicate that the initial demand would completely

The production Mk II Tiger, as it appeared on the American market. The removal of the chrome body strip tended to make the car look shorter than the Mk I. (Photo: Chrysler UK)

monopolize the Jensen production line. So, as with the Mk I before it, Rootes decided to export the entire output from the factory and satisfy the American market before introducing the car to home dealers.

AF205 and 206 were the last prototype test cars, featuring the disc/drum brakes and 13 inch wheels of the Mk I Tiger. During 1966 and early 1967, they were used for continued evaluation of the 289 cu in engine and gearbox, and to investigate the use of Firestone PR 115 radial ply tyres as an alternative to the crossply Dunlop RS5s normally fitted. These were found to be unsatisfactory.

The first Mk II Tiger was produced on 23 December 1966, bearing the chassis number B382100100. (In fact, two cars bearing the chassis numbers B382100001 and B382100002 were built on 19 December. Unfortunately, no records remain, but it is thought that these were pre-production analysis vehicles, preceding the start of series production by just four days.) In its road test, headed 'Sunbeam Tiger II', *Road and Track* began by explaining how it was that after acquiring a large share in the Rootes Group, the Chrysler Corporation found itself producing a car with an American Ford engine. *Road and Track* were glad that Chrysler had decided not to terminate production of the car, which they described as a 'fine automotive package'. They then went on to describe the differences between the two models. 'Like the Tiger I, the Tiger II is difficult to fault within the framework of what it is intended to be.' Unfortunately, the car was a lot less than it should have been as a result of having been built to a price. 'As for performance, there's more power available from the 200 bhp V8 than the Tiger can handle with complete equanimity.' Although the Panhard rod had been lowered to a new position on the chaissis, the modification was not entirely successful. However, *Road and Track* concluded their test by saying, 'If you treat it right, respect it for what it is, the Tiger II can offer driving pleasure of a very high order.'

It is interesting to note that *Road and Track's* test appeared in their September 1967 issue. Three months earlier, on 27 June 1967, Jensen had produced their last Tiger, with the chassis number B382100633. This utilized the last of the 289 cu in engines, and no more were ordered from Ford.

Initially, Chrysler had no intention of withdrawing the Tiger. As we shall see in Chapter 9, they were very enthusiastic about keeping the car in production — if a suitable Chrysler power unit could be found. For Chrysler dealers to stock Ford engines and gearbox parts was obviously not an acceptable arrangement.

Rootes were never to bring the Mk II Tiger to the British showrooms. In fact, those Tigers that were sold in Britain during 1967 were all 'old' Mk Is, as Jensen stopped producing the Mk I before embarking on the Mk II programme.

If the Chrysler UK records are correct, only 533 units were produced during the Mk II building programme. With a retail price of $3842, the production Mk II Tiger continued to offer real motoring fun and excellent value for money.

Competition

When Norman Garrad transferred to Rootes' sales department in February 1964, he brought to a close fifteen years as Rootes' competitions manager. During this period, Garrad's effectiveness and single mindedness had earned him the title of *Führer*. This was ungenerous, for Garrard had created and sustained a formidable team of drivers whose members — Mike Hawthorn, Stirling Moss, Sheila Van Damm, Peter Collins and Graham Hill among them — were world famous in their own right.

During the early days of development, Ian Garrad kept his father fully informed of the Alpine V8 project, for Norman considered that the car could be an ideal contender in the GT category of international rallies. With this in mind, Norman Garrad talked the matter over with Timothy Rootes. He agreed to an Alpine V8 competition programme and with his approval Norman then drew up a list of the events he thought most suited to the car, including the Geneva Rally and the Le Man 24 hours. But the decision to adopt the V8 as a regular competition vehicle created a problem. Who was going to carry out the specialized development work on the engines? Rootes' competitions department had no previous knowledge or experience of modifying V8 engines. Norman Garrad's solution was to ask his son (who was in Los Angeles) to contact Carroll Shelby with a view to obtaining modified units from Shelby's own workshop. Shelby was only too pleased to oblige, and an order was placed for four race-prepared 4.2 litre engines, and three further units of similar capacity suitably modified for rallying.

The Le Mans development Tiger. The rear spoiler was detachable. The body, along with those of the two race cars, was built by Williams & Pritchard, London, under sub-contract from Brian Lister. It is equipped with Dunlop alloy wheels and Dunlop racing tyres. (Photo: Chrysler UK)

Norman Garrad's replacement as competitions manager was Marcus Chambers, who took over on 17 February 1964. Chambers had been connected with international motor sport for more than thirty years, his early post-war career being with HRG. He had spent seven years as competitions manager with BMC where he was instrumental in initiating Pat Moss's rallying career. He had then left BMC for Appleyards of Bradford to take over as works manager, staying for two and a half years before joining Rootes.

On his first day with Rootes, Chambers was driven to the Stoke plant in one of the development Alpine V8s. There, he had an introductory chat with Timothy Rootes before being taken to the competitions workshop, where he met John Rowe, the competitions department's team manager, Jim Ashworth, the chief engineer and Jerry Spencer, the chief mechanic.

Clearly, entering the Alpine V8 for Le Mans was high on the list of priorities. Chambers recalled: 'I hadn't been to Le Mans for many years [so] maybe I should have walked out.' However, the project was well advanced by February 1964 and one of Chambers's first jobs was to visit Brian Lister in Cambridge for a progress report. Lister had been commissioned to build three special bodies, the first of which was to form the basis for a development vehicle. The other two were to be used as the actual race cars. When Peter Wilson first asked him to construct these race cars, Lister immediately suggested using space frames with alloy replicas of the Tiger body mounted on them, in order to save weight. But Rootes were insistent that the cars be as original as possible, accepting the penalty of the extra weight. Ron Wisdom, one of Rootes' body stylists had used a $\frac{1}{4}$ scale model in the wind tunnel at MIRA to develop the best overall shape for the Le Mans cars. Tests were then carried out to evaluate such factors as minimum drag, lift and pitching, aerodynamic stability, engine, water and oil cooling, engine compartment ventilation, interior ventilation and windscreen wiping under high speed.

All of these factors were, of course, crucial to the high speeds at which the cars were designed to travel. A rear spoiler was designed to aid the high speed traction of the rear wheels. The designers realized that this would result in a somewhat nose-light attitude and it was thus made detachable for optional use. To assist with both engine and braking ventilation, ducts were cut in the front apron of the cars so that air could reach the radiator and front wheels, while scoops were fitted under the cars to force air to the rear axle and brakes. From a graph plotting body drag against engine power, the team were able to calculate that, fitted with 260 bhp engines, the cars would be capable of 170 mph!

From his discussions with Lister, Chambers discovered that there were several problems. First, there was a general shortage of racing parts. Secondly, the special Salisbury rear axles which had been supplied were too wide. As the cars would be reaching speeds of 150 mph, 15 inch diameter wheels had been thought essential, but had they been fitted to these axles, the tyres would have fouled the bodywork. Like many other racing and rallying teams, Rootes enjoyed a close rapport with tyre manufacturers, and with Dunlop in particular. As the wheels and tyres for the Le Mans cars had yet to be purchased, Chambers arranged for

The prototype Le Mans Tiger photographed outside Rootes' competitions department. At this stage, the car still had the original exhaust system. (Photo: Marcus Chambers).

Marcus Chambers and Keith Ballisat discuss the problems with the development Le Mans race car. The front valance has been drastically cut away to increase the air flow to the radiator. The exhaust pipe diameter seems rather small. (Photo: Chrysler UK)

a Dunlop representative to call. He showed Chambers a new 15 inch magnesium alloy wheel costing £38 each. They were just what were required for the Le Mans cars, so Chambers bought 32 of them.

Unfortunately, finance, always the silent enemy of the Rootes competitions department, was rearing its ugly head. It was becoming increasingly obvious that the Le Mans cars were going to cost far more than had originally been forecast. The latest calculations indicated that the programme would cost approximately £3000 more than the original budget had allowed.

In early April 1964, three of the engines which had been ordered from Carroll Shelby in America were delivered. On Shelby's recommendation, Rootes had chosen 260 engines which had a claimed output of 275 bhp. Twin four-barrel Ford carburettors were mounted on a special manifold and a re-profiled camshaft operated solid cam followers (lifters). A dual point distributor was fitted together with heavy duty ignition leads. The cylinder heads had been modified by Shelby's engineers, and a special clutch transmitted the power to a gearbox which had an alloy casting and a close ratio gear train.

Meanwhile, the development car, registration number 7743 KV, had been completed, and was collected from Brian Lister in readiness for its first run. It featured a Salisbury limited slip differential and large Girling disc brakes all

Keith Ballisat testing the Le Mans development car. So little time was available for a concentrated test programme that the handling was never entirely satisfactory. The name 'Tiger' was removed from all photographs of this period. (Photo: Chrysler UK)

round, with independent master cylinders operating alloy calipers. An oil cooler and a 30 gallon fuel tank had also been added.

On 15 April 1964, 7743 KV was taken to Mallory Park for its first test run. The suspension had been set up using Armstrong GT dampers and the Dunlop R6 tyres were set at 50 psi. Keith Ballisat, one of the works drivers, was the first to take the car out, but soon returned to the pits. He complained of severe axle tramp, and loss of control of the rear end after hitting small bumps. As a result, the development team decided to fit dampers with harder settings on the rear to eliminate axle tramp, and harder dampers on the front to cut down float. The spring rates were increased and an anti-roll bar was fitted to reduce roll.

With these modifications completed, the car was taken to the Le Mans circuit for further testing during the test weekend on 18-19 April. Only at Le Mans could the car reach its designed maximum speed. In heavy rain, Keith Ballisat set out to test the effectiveness of the alterations. Unfortunately, the problems persisted. Even worse, new headaches appeared when the car was stretched to its limit. With the engine reaching 6000 rpm in top gear down the Mulsanne straight, the oil pressure dropped to a critical level and the radiator boiled. The handling was also disappointing. Chambers then asked Mike Parkes — the Ferrari team driver who was practising at the time — to take the V8 out and evaluate it. An ex-Rootes development engineer, Parkes echoed Ballisat's

Mike Parkes takes the wheel of the development Tiger during the Le Mans practice weekend. Watching him are (left to right): Marcus Chambers (with folder), John Rowe, Alec Caine and Peter Wilson (in dark raincoat). (Photo: Chrysler UK)

criticisms. Not only was the car's handling a severe problem, the brakes were clearly inadequate. Parkes's best Tiger lap time was 4 minutes 26.4 seconds — his Ferrari managed 3 minutes 47.1 seconds!

Later that evening, Chambers and his team set about substituting a larger radiator in the hope that it would overcome the heating difficulties, and the following day Peter Proctor took the car out to see how it performed. Later in the pits, he too complained of low oil pressure, axle tramp and inferior brakes. In an effort to improve the handling, the anti-roll bar was removed, but this had little effect. Even the larger radiator had done nothing to help.

The next outing was scheduled for 29 April at Snetterton. On this occasion the weather was more favourable and Keith Ballisat set out once more to test the effectiveness of the latest modifications. Unfortunately, the rear anti-roll bar fouled the prop shaft, so Ballisat was forced to return to the pits for adjustments. Chambers decided to remove the anti-roll bar completely and Ballisat went out again only to return minutes later. The handling was worse than ever, with excessive float and axle tramp. Next, Chambers fitted Koni rear dampers (one of the suggestions made by Mike Parkes). After a brief test, Ballisat returned saying that there had been an improvement although rear-end difficulties remained. Next, the dampers were adjusted to their hardest setting. This helped still further. The rear-end float had been eliminated, but the inner wheel continued to lift on tight corners. Chambers then simulated a revised position for the petrol tank, by draining the existing tank and placing sand bags as ballast in the new position. This done, Ballisat was sent out again, to report a further improvement. Finally, the Panhard rod was lowered by 3 inches and after a brief test, a jubilant Ballisat returned to the pits to report that the handling was even better. At this point they decided to postpone any further tests until additional spares were available.

By 12 May, the fourth 'Cobra' engine had arrived from Shelby. Two days later the development car was taken to Silverstone for its final trials. On this occasion, Keith Ballisat was accompanied by Bernard Unett, a member of Rootes' vehicle development department. Since the car's last outing at Snetterton, the front springs had been replaced by new ones having a higher spring rate, to increase front end stiffness and lessen the inner rear wheel's tendency to pick up during cornering. In case the suspension required further tuning, two new anti-roll bars were also taken along, of 1.0 inch and 1.25 inch diameter, together with a set of adjustable Koni shock absorbers (the original Koni dampers fitted at Snetterton had been replaced by Armstrong dampers).

After a considerable amount of testing, in dry but windy conditions, the Koni dampers were fitted on both front and rear. At the same time, the 13/16 inch anti-roll bar was replaced by the 1.0 inch bar, and the front springs were replaced by even stiffer versions. This done, Ballisat and Unett found the handling enormously improved. Indeed, Unett managed a best lap time of 1 minute 52 seconds. (Compare this to the 1 minute 43 seconds set in September 1976 by John Beasley, driving a 5-3 litre Corvette at an average speed of 102 mph, and the 2 minutes 4 seconds set in October 1976 by David Preece, driving a 3.8 litre XK140 Jaguar at an average speed of 84-86 mph.)

However, low oil pressure continued to cause concern and two weeks later Chambers took the development car to MIRA for further testing. A full investigation revealed that the lack of oil pressure was caused by oil flowing to the front of the crankcase, being heated and then whipped up by the crankshaft. As there was no obvious solution, the problem was left unsolved, although Chambers gave specific instructions that the sump should not be overfilled!

On 4 June 1964, Chambers went over to Cambridge to see how Listers were progressing with the two race cars. He had decided to ask Salisbury to supply new axles to stop the rear wheels fouling the bodywork. The first had already been fitted to the development car, but further supplies were late in arriving and had set Listers back at least two weeks. This left little time in hand to finish the cars, and only a matter of days to transport them back to Coventry, trim the interiors and finalize preparations for the race.

The four drivers chosen to compete in the Le Mans cars were Peter Proctor, Jimmy Blumer, Keith Ballisat and Claude Dubois. Proctor had begun his racing career in 1956 and partnered Peter Harper in the 1961 Le Mans. Jimmy

Blummer started his career in 1950, and in 1962 won the Brands Hatch International 6 hours with Mike Parkes. Keith Ballisat, the competitions manager for Shell Oil, also had racing successes to his credit, having twice won a Coupe des Alpes in the Alpine Rally. Claude Dubois, a Belgian, possessed invaluable experience too, having competed at Le Mans on four occasions.

The four drivers were to be paired as follows:

Claude Dubois and Keith Ballisat	ADU 179B (car No. 8)
Jimmy Blumer and Peter Proctor	ADU 180B (car No. 9)

On Monday, 15 July, the two brand new and as yet untried Le Mans Tigers were flown out from Hurn Airport. Their departure was delayed as they had been late in arriving from Coventry. The following day, both cars were taken through scrutineering where there was a hold-up because car No. 8 had been fitted with a different, but nevertheless identical engine to the one which had been listed in the RAC homologation papers. By late afternoon, the cars had been cleared, their tanks filled with petrol and final preparations were being made for the next day.

On Wednesday, practice day, car No. 8 ran its main bearings, after having covered only one and a half laps, and had to be wheeled away. Not long after, Peter Proctor, driving car No. 9, returned to the pits complaining that there was a lack of performance. Apparently, the car would not exceed 5000 rpm in top gear. Moreover, although it was not reaching maximum speed, the oil pressure was still low. Later that evening, the engine in car No. 8 was changed in readiness for the next day's practice.

After so many setbacks, there was a feeling of disquiet and disappointment in the team. The general opinion was that there had been too little time to locate and cure all the problems. In addition, most of the team members agreed that, had such details as plugs, coil, oil cooler and carburettor float level received fuller attention, the cars would probably have been running better. Clearly, Chambers was a worried man. This was his first time back at Le Mans after many years, and as the new competitions manager he was obviously concerned about team morale and performance. And of course Rootes were hoping that the race would provide good publicity, which would help to launch the Sunbeam Tiger in America.

On Thursday morning, in despair, Chambers rang Peter Wilson in Coventry. He recounted the setbacks and asked Wilson, 'Wouldn't it be sensible to retire now?' Wilson pointed out that much time and money had been devoted to the work and urged Chambers to carry on, which he did.

In his role as spectator and technical adviser to the Rootes team, Lister had been right about the weight of the Tiger bodies, for this factor told heavily against them. At some 2640 lb (66 lb heavier than the standard models), they

The two Sunbeam Tigers in position for the start of the race. Both cars were completely untried, as lack of time had precluded any testing. (Photo: Chrysler UK)

were the second heaviest cars in the race, weighing 160 lb more than the Shelby Cobras (which had the larger 4.7 litre engines, developing about 100 bhp more than the Tiger).

To Chambers's bitter disappointment, the Tigers were quite overwhelmed. Car No. 8 retired with piston failure, although it had managed a maximum speed of 161.6 mph along the Mulsanne straight during its three hours on the track. Its overall position ranged between 26th and 32nd. Car No. 9 did better, lasting nine hours before a broken crankshaft forced it to retire. It had completed 123 laps

Car no 9, photographed just before it retired. Note the quick lift jacking points.
(Photo: Chrysler UK)

averaging approximately 107 mph, with a fastest speed of 162.2 mph down the Mulsanne straight. Its overall position was as high as 18th during its last hour. Its petrol consumption was 8.5 mpg.

Tiger

Car no 8 during the early stages of the race. It finally retired with piston failure.
(Photo: Chrysler UK)

Car no 8 — enveloped by smoke and out of the race. It had completed only three hours of racing out of the twenty-four.

Most motoring journalists agreed that the Tigers appeared to handle badly, despite the effort that had been spent in their preparation. In fact, one magazine noted that, for the other drivers, overtaking the Tigers was the most hazardous aspect of the race! Paradoxically, Ballisat considers that 'the handling qualities of the Le Mans cars were first class for the Le Mans circuit'.

The winner of the 1964 Le Mans was a 3.3 litre Ferrari while a Shelby Cobra finished fourth, proving that there was nothing wrong with Ford's V8. For Chambers, it had been a regrettable experience, and for Rootes, an expensive failure. However, rumour suggests that Shelby's engine test bed had been out of action during the period in which he developed the Rootes engines: possibly two of these units had not undergone sufficiently rigorous bench testing. In any event, the failure of the Le Mans Tiger engines was attributed to slack tolerances, which in Chambers's opinion also accounted for the low oil pressure. 'When we confronted Shelby with the problem,' said Chambers, 'he was not willing to comment and it was not until Rootes applied certain pressure that we were refunded.'

Rootes' experience with the team of Sunbeam Tigers at the 1964 Le Mans 24 Hours had been regrettable. The cars had received considerable adverse publicity and it was decided there and then that all future competition effort should be concentrated upon rallying.

In early May, a representative from Tech Del Ltd had walked into the competitions workshop to show Chambers the 'Minilite' magnesium wheel which his company was currently marketing. Chambers had heard that the Minilite was gaining a reputation with other rally competitors for strength and reliability and he immediately bought some. The 13 inch 5J wheels were offered at just over £11 each.

To search out the weak points of the Tiger under rally conditions, Chambers arranged a trip to France for 12 July. As none of the rally cars had been completed by then, Chambers, Jerry Spencer and one of the works drivers, Tiny Lewis, set off in one of the Rootes development Tigers. Unfortunately, the trip had its fair share of misfortunes. In France, the car hit a rock which damaged the front wing and broke the Panhard bracket on the rear axle. Repairs had to be carried out at a local garage before the car could continue. The following day was spent at Mont Ventoux to test the brakes and cooling. After a fast run up, the engine temperature continued to rise which inevitably caused boiling. Removing the chrome grille bar effected a cure, allowing just that extra amount of air to pass through to the radiator and prevent it from boiling. Soon after testing had started, Lewis complained that the car's handling had become vague, and an investigation indicated worn dampers. Further problems were in store the next day: a fire started in the main battery lead and later, during a fast test run, the Tiger hit a Renault saloon, which meant that a recovery vehicle had to be called out to tow it to the nearest garage for repairs.

By the beginning of July, the first rally Tiger, ADU 311B, had been completed by the competitions workshop. This was one of three cars that were to be entered in the Geneva Rally in October. Before this, however, the car had to be taken to the Smith's instruments factory, Cricklewood, London, to have a tachometer fault investigated.

Later in the month, Rosemary Smith and Peter Riley took the car on a survey or recce trip to France in preparation for the rally. Such recces had originally been introduced to the team by Norman Garrad. Sending a car over the course in advance of a rally enabled valuable information regarding routes and speeds to be collected and passed on to the rest of the team before the actual event.

Rosemary Smith has particularly fond memories of her association with the Tiger: 'While Peter Riley and I were on the recceing trip in France, he said, "You know, you and Tigers get on very well together." . . . I was sorry that Rootes did not allow me to enter more events with the Tiger. I felt it was a very relaxing car to drive in comparison to the Imp which I used a lot, later. One always had to work so hard in the Imp, using first and second gear all the time, and it got so noisy too, but then Rootes wanted my name to become synonymous with Imps, so that was that.'

By September, all three cars, ADU 310B, ADU 311B, and ADU 312B, had been completed and were ready for their first international rally the following

Rosemary Smith (left) and Margaret MacKenzie with their Tiger at the beginning of the 1964 Geneva Rally. (Photo: Chrysler UK)

month. The engines were those supplied by Carroll Shelby's workshops in Venice, California. These were 4.2-litre units with Holley carburettors, modified camshafts, solid cam followers, and modified cylinder heads. The clutches were also Shelby units, while the Ford gearboxes had special Warner close ratios. Rootes' competitions workshop had added Salisbury Powr-Lok differentials, which had 3.77:1 ratios and oil coolers for the engines. The suspensions incorporated export Husky springs and Rapier rally dampers, together with 0.75 inch stabilizer bars. The brakes had harder pads and linings, and 26-gallon fuel tanks were fitted. Minilite wheels were used in place of the steel versions, plus the obligatory spot lamps.

On 13 October, the three cars set off to rendezvous in Arbois for the start of the rally. The Geneva always attracted special interest in the rally world, not just because it was a tough, exciting and well-organized event, but because it was decisive in the European championship. Clearly, the 1250 mile event was going to prove a probing testing ground for the new Tigers.

The problems, however, began even before the start. Peter Riley's car gave considerable trouble on the way to Arbois. Fortunately, this proved to be nothing more than defective ignition contact points, but Tiny Lewis's car had meanwhile developed clutch problems. When the mechanics removed the gearbox to investigate, they discovered that the linings were completely burnt out. A new clutch was essential, and so the mechanics worked all night to replace the linings. This work delayed the car for scrutineering. However, it was through by 11.00 am and all three cars had set off safely by early evening.

Towards the closing stages of the rally, fan belt problems were plaguing all three Tigers. As a result Chambers instructed Rosemary, Tiny and Peter to drive a little slower and aim for a class win. But there were problems with the tyres too. Because the Dunlop service van was late in arriving at a scheduled stop, the cars had to continue on their original tyres.

Nevertheless, the Tigers finished 11th, 15th, and 20th overall and scored a 1-2-3 victory in the over 2500 cc GT class.

In early November 1964, AHP 483B, a works team Tiger, was entered in the RAC Rally. Driven by the Revd Rupert Jones and John Clegg, this was one of two works cars built during this period. (The second was AHP 295B, which was used in the 1965 Monte Carlo Rally and later as an Alpine Rally recce car.)

Revd Rupert Jones and John Clegg during the early part of the 1964 RAC Rally. Note the sump guard and steel wheels. (Photo: Chrysler UK)

Revd Rupert Jones struggles to keep the Tiger on the track during a speed section of the RAC Rally. (Photo: Chrysler UK)

Possibly as a result of the failure of the Shelby-prepared engines at Le Mans, the engines for these two cars were bought direct from Ford in Detroit. They featured modified cylinder heads, reprofiled camshafts, and solid lifters. Bench testing indicated that one engine produced 211 bhp at 5200 rpm and the other 217 bhp at 5000 rpm. The rally started in treacherous weather at the Duke of York Barracks, Chelsea. Unfortunately, on the second night, while completing a rough special stage, Jones's Tiger went off the road and thus failed to finish.

In November 1964, the Rootes' competitions department had the good fortune to employ Des O'Dell. O'Dell had gained vast experience at Aston Martin (where he had been chief tester for eleven years), and at Ford Advanced Vehicles, Slough, where he had helped develop the highly successful GT40s. O'Dell remembers with irony and affection his association with Rootes and the Tiger:

'If someone had told me that one day I would work for Rootes, I would have laughed in their face. Nevertheless, I came to Rootes to find these funny things called Sunbeam Tigers. They had been to Le Mans but had used the 4.2-litre engines when they could easily have had 4.7 units developed to the same extent as the GT40s. But then I found out that it had been Carroll Shelby who had suggested using the smaller engine and by so doing giving away about 100 bhp.

'I just employed my GT40 experience to make the Tiger more reliable, using 289 crankshafts and rods because they were so much stronger and which I was able to buy direct from Ford at Slough.

'But initially, cooling was a problem. When I first came I had several discussions with the slide-rule boffins, chaps who had never sat inside a car in their lives. They told me that I should raise the engine by one inch and move it back in the frame one inch and use a larger fan. Well, I would have preferred not to use a fan at all, and as for raising the centre of gravity . . .!

'The problem was that the car overheated even on early morning runs down the motorway, so it was definitely going to overheat on something like the Acropolis Rally. Using one of the development cars, I would go for a run down the motorway, and open it up to 120 mph but within six miles it would boil!

The interior of Rootes' competitions department, with ADU 312B in the background. Initially, Rootes bought tuned engines for their rally cars from Carroll Shelby. (Photo: Chrysler UK)

Anyway, I did some checks and found that the air was passing through everywhere but the radiator, so I instructed the engineers to put in more air ducts. Then I remembered that Aston Martin and Mercedes had suffered from similar problems, and that they had been cured by the alteration of the header tank arrangement, so I repiped the Tiger to match the Mercedes layout. I took a pipe from the header tank to the bottom hose, a modification the boffins said would never work, and tried again. I took it on the motorway, tucking in behind a lorry until it boiled, then broke free and went like hell, and the temperature went down. I had cured the problem in three weeks! On some occasions we ran with the bonnets open to increase the air flow. We also lowered the suspension using Koni dampers and introduced dual circuit braking . . . On tarmac, it was most impressive, but it was just never any good on forest rallies.'

In January 1965, Rootes entered two Tigers and three Hillman Imps in the 2600 mile Monte Carlo Rally. Andrew Cowan and Robin Turvey were to drive AHP 295B (this was Cowan's first entry in the Monte with a competitive car), while Peter Harper and Ian Hall were to drive ADU 312B. The cars featured special heated screens front and rear and de-icing jets.

Harper and Hall press on in the 1965 Monte Carlo Rally. The hole in the front wing is to help cooling. (Photo: Chrysler UK)

Andrew Cowan and Robin Turvey in a characteristically snowy section of the 1965 Monte. (Photo: Chrysler UK)

The 1965 Monte is remembered most for its exceptionally bad weather conditions. Of the 237 starters, only 35 arrived at Monte Carlo, having survived the treacherous snow-covered mountain sections starting at St Claude. In his book *Why Finish Last?* Andrew Cowan recalls that the drive as far as St Claude was without major problems although he was troubled by a locking handbrake. He duly persuaded a local village mechanic to modify the handbrake into a 'fly-off' type. This cured the problem and he was then able to hang the tail out to increase his cornering speeds, although he later discovered that it would not stay on when the car was parked!

When the cars arrived at Monte Carlo, Harper and Cowan were lying first and second in their class. Marcus Chambers felt that Harper — with his greater experience — should aim for the highest possible placing overall, so Cowan was instructed to 'take it easy' to increase Rootes' chances of a class win. However, Cowan's own moment of glory came when he won the driving test on the front at Monte Carlo the following morning. Their overall placings were: Harper fourth, and Cowan eleventh.

Peter Harper and Ian Hall receive their trophies for the 1975 Monte. The overall placings were: Harper, fourth; Cowan, eleventh. (Photo: Chrysler UK)

The start of the 1965 Tulip Rally. Rootes entered two Sunbeam Tigers, driven by Peter Riley and Peter Harper. (Photo: Autocar)

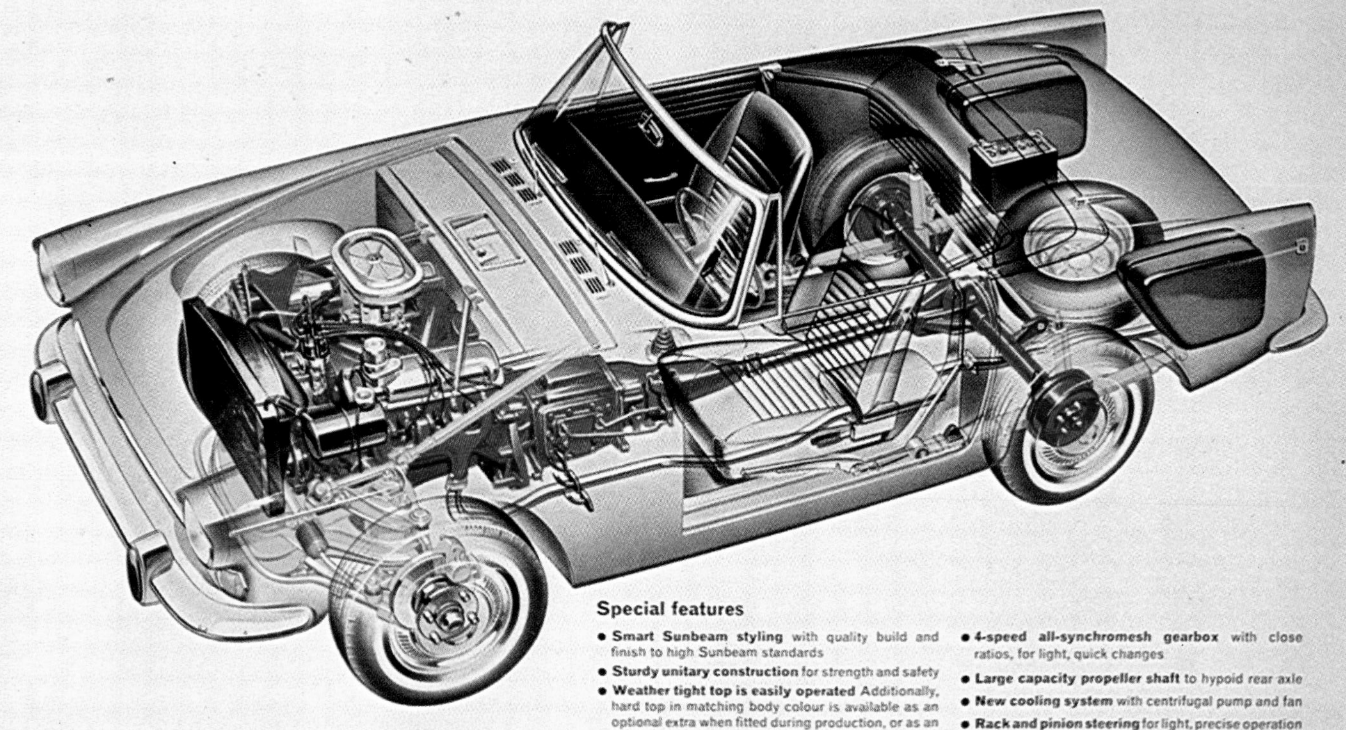

A BRILLIANT PRODUCT OF ADVANCED DESIGN

Special features

- **Smart Sunbeam styling** with quality build and finish to high Sunbeam standards
- **Sturdy unitary construction** for strength and safety
- **Weather tight top is easily operated** Additionally, hard top in matching body colour is available as an optional extra when fitted during production, or as an accessory in black only.
- **Vacuum servo-assisted braking** with self-adjusting front disc brakes
- **V8 power unit for sporting performance** Compact, lightweight 8-cylinder engine of short stroke, low-friction design
- **Engine features** include: twin-barrel carburettor with automatic choke, dual exhaust system
- **10 in. (254 mm.) diameter clutch,** hydraulically operated, with centrifugal assistance
- **4-speed all-synchromesh gearbox** with close ratios, for light, quick changes
- **Large capacity propeller shaft** to hypoid rear axle
- **New cooling system** with centrifugal pump and fan
- **Rack and pinion steering** for light, precise operation
- **No greasing points** – simplified maintenance
- **Powerful, double-dip headlights** for night safety
- **Road-speed, nylon-corded tyres** for high speed travel
- **Twin fuel tanks,** total capacity – 11½ gallons (51 litres)
- **67 amp battery** for all electrical needs
- **Large luggage compartment,** 9¼ cu. ft. (0·262 cu. m.) capacity

Another of the five pre-production Mk II Tigers. This car is owned by an Australian who had it shipped out after purchasing it in Britain. (Photo: A. Ford)

Peter Riley on the Tulip Rally, taking care not to apply too much power during a heavy snow storm. Both Tigers retired from the rally, because of the bad weather. (Photo: Chrysler UK)

For the 1965 Tulip Rally held in April, Rootes entered Peter Harper and Peter Riley, both driving Tigers, and Rosemary Smith and Tiny Lewis in Hillman Imps. Unfortunately for the Tigers, the weather was so bad that both Harper and Riley were forced to retire as all the sections had been badly hit by snow. On

John Gott and D. E. Nicholson on the 1965 International Police Rally. They finished first overall after an excellent drive. (Photo: Autocar)

one particular hill, the Tigers just failed to reach the top. However, Rosemary showed the superiority of the Imp under such conditions and went on to an outright victory, winning the Coupe Des Dames at the same time. Tiny Lewis finished second.

Towards the end of April, John Gott telephoned Marcus Chambers to ask if he could borrow a works Tiger. Over lunch, he explained to Marcus that he wanted to compete in the International Police Rally in Belgium. Marcus agreed, and on 29 May, Gott set off in AHP 295B on the 690 mile circular route across Belgium. The 93 starters, including both civilian and military police teams from seven countries, started and finished in Liége. Gott and his co-driver, D. E. Nicholson, not only finished first overall, but were the only team to finish the road section unpenalized and set the fastest times in two of the hill climbs.

ANOTHER RALLY VICTORY FOR ROOTES

Outright win for

SUNBEAM TIGER

International Police Rally 1965

BY APPOINTMENT TO
HER MAJESTY THE QUEEN
MOTOR VEHICLE
MANUFACTURERS
ROOTES MOTORS LTD.

Results subject to official confirmation.

ROOTES MOTORS LIMITED

LONDON SHOWROOMS AND EXPORT DIVISION
ROOTES LIMITED DEVONSHIRE HOUSE PICCADILLY LONDON W1

690 miles against 92 other cars – without a single penalty point!

Driven by John Gott, Chief Constable of Northants, navigated by Sgt. D. E. Nicholson.

The Sunbeam Tiger's victory is a resounding one. Starting and finishing in Liege, Belgium, May 29-30, and competing against civilian and military police teams from seven countries, **the Tiger was the only car to finish the 24-hour rally unpenalised in the road section, while on two of the speed hill climbs it established the fastest recorded times.** That's the rally-winning form of the Sunbeam Tiger that takes it way out in front with sports enthusiasts.

Tiger top in USA, too! Santa Barbara Road Races, California, May 29th, Sunbeam Tiger driven to top place in Class B Production race by Jim Adams for Hollywood Sports Cars – 135 mph on the straight, average speed 101 mph.

Advertisement from Autocar, *11 June 1965, celebrating the Tiger's overall win in the 1965 International Police Rally.*

A battered but nevertheless competitive Tiger in the 49th Targa Florio. Sponsored by British Vitafoam, and driven by Harper and Jones, this car featured a Cobra 4.7 litre engine which put it into the prototype category. (Photo: Geoffrey Goddard)

Vitafoam entered a Sunbeam Tiger in the 1965 Targa Florio. Driven by Peter Harper and the Revd Rupert Jones, this was a specially modified works rally car, featuring a 4.7 litre 'Cobra' engine with a 4 barrel Holley, ducted cooling to the rear brakes exhausting through the boot, and over-size wheels and tyres. Because of its engine specification, it was entered in the prototype category where it finished second! Initially, the car was relegated to an unclassified position because the time difference between it and the winner in class, a Ferrari 275PZ, was greater than 15 per cent. Three weeks later this ruling was refuted and the Tiger was confirmed as second in class.

The Tiger had thus gained a good reputation in the rally world by the time the production cars were released in the United Kingdom. But its weight, and in particular the fact that most of it was concentrated over the front wheels, was still its greatest handicap, especially on special stages. Although the suspension was able to withstand the rigours of day-to-day driving, it developed weaknesses when subjected to the extra strains of a rally. Moreover, the engineers found that the

The Harper/Jones Tiger undergoes roadside repairs in the Targa Florio. It was finally confirmed in second place in the prototype class. (Photo: Geoffrey Goddard)

V8 unit left little free space in the engine compartment, making roadside repairs particularly difficult.

The next rally on the Rootes calendar was the Scottish, which took place in June 1965. This was the Tiger's first forest event. Although the weather was good, Paddy Hopkirk described it as 'the roughest, toughest rally I have ever been on'. Covering 1700 miles of mountainous terrain, with 290 miles of special stages, the rally demanded flat-out motoring over cross-country track on private land. Of the 102 starters, only 43 competitors lasted the course, the Imps of Rosemary Smith and Tiny Lewis finishing second and fifth respectively overall.

Andrew Cowan in one of the works Sunbeam Tigers was not so lucky. Unable to cope with the rough surfaces, the front suspension collapsed, then the exhaust pipes fell off, and the oil filter leaked oil over the universal joint in the steering column. Eventually, all the oil leaked away and Cowan had to stop a passing competitor for assistance. He turned out to be a fellow Scot and only too willing to help. With some more oil in the sump, Cowan was able to limp to the next control point where he met Marcus Chambers. Chambers took one look at the front suspension, which had been tied up with wire, and decided that Cowan should withdraw. It later transpired that when Cowan had filled up with oil after his accident with the filter, he inadvertently mixed castor-based oil with vegetable oil — with dire results! The second Tiger, EGA 65C, driven by John Melvin and Hamish Wilson, was also very badly battered. At one stage the boot lid popped open, spilling tools all over the road. It did manage to stay the course, however, and won the over-2500cc class for GT cars.

The Alpine Rally (which in previous years had suffered its fair share of problems) followed later that month. For Rootes and the Sunbeam Tigers it was arguably their most publicized event — not because of Harper's victory on the road, but because of his subsequent disqualification. The rally lasted a total of 5½ days and covered a distance of 2250 miles from Marseilles to Monte Carlo. The Rootes works Tigers were driven by Peter Harper (ADU 312B), Tiny Lewis (ADU 311B), and Ian Hall (AHP 295B) deputizing for Peter Riley at short notice. On a dull and overcast evening, the 93 cars prepared to leave Marseilles on the first stage to Grenoble. Quite early on, Harper's starter motor jammed, but the resourceful Jerry Spencer made arrangements to replace the faulty unit at the next control point. As Harper roared up, the mechanics started work only to be interrupted by Chambers. 'What's going on?' he asked. 'You haven't enough time to change the starter motor.' But it was too late. While Chambers and Des O'Dell had been arguing, the mechanics had finished the job and Harper was on his way!

A short breathing space on the 1965 Alpine Rally — possibly the most controversial rally as far as Rootes and the Tiger were concerned. (Photo: Chrysler UK)

Magnificent scenery on the Alpine Rally. Harper won the GT category, only to be disqualified because of a homologation problem. (Photo: Autocar)

Ian Hall was the first of the Tiger contingent to go out of the rally, suffering from brake trouble. He was not the only one, for in the words of O'Dell, 'both Harper and Lewis were using brake pads like they were going out of fashion.' In fact, Harper was trying to perfect a new braking technique, using both the accelerator and the handbrake to achieve the best line through corners. 'We had to use three service crews just to keep Harper going', continued Des. Later, Tiny's car came in to have the rear brakes adjusted. Unfortunately, a complete lining came away from the shoe, allowing the piston to pop out and causing brake fluid to spray over the red hot drum. The fluid immediately caught fire, but luckily caused little damage. Lewis crashed later on and this put him out of the rally.

Harper had an excellent rally and was initially placed first overall in the GT category. With this reassuring news, O'Dell went to bed. However, his slumbers were soon disturbed when he was summoned to the scrutineering garage. The French officials had the bonnet of Harper's car open and were measuring the valve sizes in the cylinder heads. They wrote down the results on a piece of paper, drew a line and went over to the homologation sheets where they wrote down the valve size shown in the data. An official did this twice, then walked up to O'Dell and told him that Harper's car was disqualified. O'Dell went back to the hotel to tell Harper the news. 'Peter wanted to buy me a drink,' recalls Des, 'but it was no good, I just had to tell him he had been disqualified. I wouldn't want to live those ten minutes again.' Harper had won his class only to be robbed of victory over a point of detail.

Although Rootes had used standard valve sizes, they were smaller than the ones shown in the homologation sheets. The French officials argued that Rootes had detuned for reliability. Later, an official statement was issued by the Rootes public relations department: 'By fitting smaller valves to the Tiger, we certainly did not gain any advantage in performance, and this was only done to bring the rally car specification into line with that of current models. The discrepancy arose because the initial production Tigers registered with the FIA were produced for the US market and employed larger valves than those currently fitted to production models. Negotiations are in progress with the FIA to register

Jerry Spencer at work on Harper's Tiger after the finish of the 1965 Alpine Rally. (Photo: Autosport)

Peter Harper's Tiger before the start of the RAC Rally, 1965. Like Revd Rupert Jones the year before, he was forced to retire. (Photo: C. Harrington)

the latest specification, but in any case we believe that it was not vital to notify a modification which detunes the engine performance.'

As O'Dell said, 'This taught me always to homologate the standard production model.'

In November 1965, Peter Harper and Peter Riley were among the 163 starters in the tough RAC Rally. Entered by Rootes, the two drivers were determined that their Tigers should avenge the 1964 performance of Jones and Clegg. Unfortunately, Riley crashed in the early stages, leaving Harper to struggle on. His stint was to be short-lived too: during the fourth stage (in fact the third, as the first was cancelled) he holed his radiator; then, on the following day, he finished a forest stage with a flat right-side front tyre; and later still, a crash finally put him out of the rally.

Because of the short supply of right-hand drive cars, the competitions department were still using left-hand drive Tigers towards the end of 1965!

The Monte Carlo Rally held in January 1966 will probably be remembered by most people for the uproar caused by the number of lighting infringements discovered during the scrutineering after the rally. The homologation rules had made the Tiger very competitive in the GT category but reduced its chances of winning overall due to the 18 per cent time handicap that had been imposed. Rootes entered two Tigers: AHP 294B, driven by Peter Harper, and FRW 667C,

Cowan and Coyle at Dover, just before boarding the ferry. Note the heated front windscreen. (Photo: United Press)

driven by Andrew Cowan. The engine in Cowan's car had been fitted with a high lift camshaft and a two-barrel Ford carburettor, and developed approximately 200 bhp. As for previous rallies, the cars were equipped with alternators and windscreen heaters, and the spring rates and damper settings were all revised. (Cowan's car, FRW 667C, was one of three built at this time, the others being FRW 668C and ERW 729C.)

The weather during the entire rally was bitterly cold, and heavy snowfalls along the route made driving hazardous. On the second day, Cowan crashed shortly after leaving Boulogne. While negotiating one of the early stages, and going quite slowly, he went over a bridge and into a corner. It seems that the car started to slide towards the verge and its front cross member then hit something

Andrew Cowan and Brian Coyle at the start of the 1966 Monte Carlo Rally. 'The best Tiger we ever built', recalled Des O'Dell.

Harper sleeps while Hall takes the wheel, in the 1966 Monte. This is the easy bit, especially with a Gendarme to show you the way. (Photo: Chrysler UK)

Harper going in fine style. Not long afterwards, the fan came forward, hitting the radiator and putting the car out of the rally. (Photo: Chrysler UK)

buried in the snow, causing the car to somersault end over end. The result was a badly dented Tiger and a very unhappy Marcus Chambers. In fact, for Marcus, the rally was a double disappointment because not long afterwards Harper retired when the fan came forward and hit the radiator, ruining the cooling system!

In April 1966 a solitary Tiger, FRW 668C, driven by Peter Harper, competed in the Tulip Rally. In previous years the marking system had been fairly complex, but for 1966 the organizers decided to make things easier, saying that the winner would simply be the quickest car.

Harper's car had been fitted with a high lift camshaft, solid lifters, extra strong valve springs, and polished cylinder heads. While the carburation had been left standard, a competition distributor had been added along with an oil cooler. Des O'Dell's ingenious dual circuit braking system featured twin servos, the second mounted on the rear seat. The 3.7:1 final drive and limited slip Powr-Lok differential transmitted the power to the rear wheels.

Harper at his best, matching his driving skill to the power of the Tiger. Note the intercom device fitted to his helmet, enabling him to talk to his co-driver above the noise of the engine. (Photo: Autocar)

Under favourable conditions, Harper managed a first in the GT category and a first in the over 2500 cc class. During the last part of the rally he had to keep hanging on to the steering wheel, for the adjustable mechanism would not lock into position.

For the 1966 Acropolis Rally, Harper's Tiger (ADU 311B) was probably at the peak of its development. Benefiting from experience gained on previous rallies, the car featured all the proven modifications together with an enormous sump guard and twin electric fans fitted to the radiator. As it turned out, the fans were unnecessary as a sufficient flow of air passed through the radiator.

Chambers flew out to Athens on 23 May where he met all the crews except Harper and Cowan, who were still away completing the recce. After spending a considerable amount of time clearing the cars through customs, Chambers and the engineers checked them over. They were due at scrutineering on 25 May in readiness for the start later that same day.

During the first stage, the throttle pedal of Harper's car jammed open, forcing him to drive the 10 kilometres to the next control point with only the ignition switch as a means of checking the engine. By the second day, all the drivers were suffering from fatigue due to the heat and dust, but the thoughtful Chambers had set up a service point at a Shell depot. This paid dividends, for Harper complained of some wheel balance problems. With the technical support of Shell available, these were soon dealt with.

Harper finished the rally in seventh overall position, winning the over 2500 cc class and coming second in the GT category. Rosemary Smith finished third in the GT category and won the Coupe des Dames with her Imp.

Harper and Hall back in ADU 311B for the Acropolis Rally. A standard bonnet replaced the vented type used in earlier rallies. Rosemary Smith is just behind in her Imp. (Photo: Autosport)

Dust and heat were a great problem in the 1966 Acropolis Rally. This was the Tiger's last rally.

The 1966 Acropolis Rally marked the end of the works Tigers' involvement in international rallying. The Hillman Imp had shown itself to be both more versatile and, on many occasions, a more successful competitor than the V8 sports car. Because of this, the factory never had the opportunity to use Mk II Tigers, although, inevitably, they would have suffered the same weight penalty as the earlier cars. Clearly, Des O'Dell's involvement with the Tiger made the car more competitive. Arguably, the Le Mans cars would have been more successful had he joined Rootes at an earlier stage. As it was, the competition department continued to concentrate their efforts on the Imp and later the Hunter.

What was it like to drive one of these rally prepared Tigers? In *Road and Track,* Henry Manney III described his driving experience with ADU 312B, which had just come back from the 1965 Monte Carlo Rally. With its multitude of lights, its lowered suspension and its Minilite wheels, it looked unmistakably like a works rally car. Inside, a pair of Heuers, one a stop watch and the other a master clock, were mounted on the passenger's side of the dashboard above the Halda Twin Master. On the driver's side, the only alteration was the addition of a larger rev-counter (red lined at 6000) mounted on top of the dashboard. This was in place of the panel-mounted version which had been disconnected. The standard Microcell seats gave good lateral support as ever, and adequate legroom for covering long distances. Manney's opinion of driving ADU 312B was summed up in one word — 'stimulating' — and he pointed out that there was a progressive delivery of power up to maximum revs.

As one might have expected from a car which had covered a high mileage as a works rally competitor, it emitted many squeaks and groans, while its exhaust was noisier than normal. Apart from its heavier clutch, hardish ride, and brakes which needed a heftier jab, its competition mechanicals were not directly apparent.

With vague steering and a flattish ride up to and beyond the cornering speeds at which Manney was prepared to drive, the car clearly demanded respect. The limited-slip differential called for a scientific approach when negotiating sharp bends, and adequate bursts of power in third gear were needed to produce the desired results.

For the best acceleration runs, the throttle had to be held at 2500 rpm. With anything less, the revs just died away as the clutch was let in, while with too many revs the rear wheels spun, losing valuable seconds from lost traction. From then on, a wary eye had to be kept on the rev counter as 6000 rpm was reached with ease in the intermediate gears. Top speed runs were limited by the rev limit imposed, but even then, with the Tiger still accelerating hard in fourth gear, the car remained stable. The only real indication of imminent maximum speed was the terrific noise which filtered through from the engine compartment.

Cars and Car Conversions tested Peter Harper's 1966 Tulip Rally car, FRW 668C. This was obviously a younger vehicle than Henry Manney's test car, but significantly, many of the comments made about ADU 312B were also raised with FRW 668C.

A modified engine coupled with a lower than normal final drive ratio (3.7:1) resulted in a car which was undoubtedly built for speed and acceleration, as the intrepid testers discovered. In fact, they soon realized that FRW 668C was most unsuited to town driving. If the revs were allowed to drop below 2000, the engine began running on only six or seven cylinders. Third gear proved to be the best for normal motoring, and was good for about 100 mph at maximum rpm. Even then, the low final drive resulted in an awful lot of power at any speed, and the throttle pedal had to be treated with respect. FRW 668C was also noisy. However, it handled well, giving a great deal of controllability. Adequate use of the throttle and steering allowed the car to be driven hard, and if a corner proved to be sharper than originally thought, a dab on the accelerator and a flick of the wheel soon had it back on line.

In addition to the noise, firm ride, and vivid acceleration, these works rally cars had one big snag — high fuel consumption. Driven with consideration, they would still return only 15 mpg approximately. With adequate use of the throttle, this was reduced to a mere 12 mpg. Presumably, this was never a worry to Mr Harper!

In addition to rallying, the Sunbeam Tiger set some new speed records, as Des O'Dell recalls. 'In early 1965, the Dutch decided to enter a Tiger in the Dutch National 24 Hours at the Zandvort circuit, as a publicity campaign for the new car. Rootes' competitions department supplied a works rally car which was driven by Rob Slotemaker and David Van Lennop, and between them they covered 1792 miles. Unfortunately, the car boiled its head off, and by 8 o'clock in the evening we were having to pit stop every 10 laps to fill up with water. Anyway, the car set some new records and, apart from the cooling problems, it went well. After the run, it was sealed up for scrutineering the following day. However, later on, the official contacted me and said he was surprised to learn that the car was fitted with different valve sizes to those shown in the homologation sheets. Luckily, Rootes had sent a car over for display purposes and, to clear up the misunderstanding, I took the official along to the showroom, removed the cylinder heads and proved that the car we had raced was fitted with identical valves to the ones in the car on display. After that, the official was willing to let the records stand and we all breathed a sigh of relief.'

Possibly the man who knows most about track racing Sunbeam Tigers is Bernard Unett. Unett had worked for Rootes since his apprenticeship and started his racing career in the early 1960s with a Sunbeam Alpine which he developed in his spare time. With this car he won the Freddie Dixon Trophy in 1964.

Unett recalls: 'At the time of the Le Mans Tigers, I was working in the experimental department, and, of course, became involved with their testing. Then, in November 1964, Marcus Chambers offered me a Le Mans car (ADU 180B) to use as the basis for a race car.

'The two other Lister-built Le Mans cars were left in Rootes' competitions workshop for some time and eventually sold off. I gutted it, rearranged the rear

The line-up for the Redex Trophy Race at Silverstone. Bernard Unett is in the foreground.

Bernard Unett at the wheel, during the Scott Brown Memorial Trophy, Snetterton, in late June 1965. (Photo: Motorsport)

suspension using full parallel locating links, altered the bonnet line, made holes for extra cooling, and fitted wide Dunlop tyres. By the start of the 1965 season I had completed the car and had begun entering races, where I found myself up against Brian Redman's E-type Jaguar, and Tony Sergeant's Merlyn, both of which I could beat. This led to good publicity. Then, in mid-season, I changed to a 289 cu. in. (4.7-litre) engine. It was fitted with twin choke Weber carburettors and produced about 360 bhp. The first time out, I took the car to Croft where, unfortunately, things got a little out of hand. Just when I was in the lead, the bonnet came up. I couldn't see where I was going, and eventually I found myself running over straw bales.'

Later in the year Bernard entered the *Autosport* Championship Final held at Snetterton. In the front line of the grid for the first heat were Tony Lanfranchi's Elva-BMW and Bernard Unett's Tiger. After a false start, Unett's pit crew took the opportunity of replenishing the Tiger's fuel tanks. On the second start attempt, all went well, and by the third lap Lanfranchi was lapping the tail-enders closely followed by Unett. Then a cruel stroke of fate forced the Tiger into the pits with a broken fan belt. This left Lanfranchi with a magnificent lead which he held until the last lap when he, too, retired. (His engine had thrown a con rod through the cylinder block.) This left Syd Taylor, driving a Brabham-Climax BT8, the surprised winner. Tony Sergeant in the Merlyn was second.

For the second heat, only nineteen starters made the grid, the others finding

The St John Trophy at Brands Hatch, August 1965. (Photo: Motorsport)

The Tiger being pursued by an AC Cobra during a meeting at Silverstone, late July 1965. (Photo: Motorsport)

the three hours between races insufficient time in which to prepare their cars. The final was started at 7 o'clock, so that the 65 laps would extend into darkness by about 1½ hours. This gave the spectators the chance of seeing the cars competing with their headlights on.

The intervening three hours had enabled Unett's team to replace the faulty fan belt, top up the radiator, and check the braking system which included adjusting the front-rear braking ratio which had given trouble earlier. As they set off, Syd Taylor's Climax went into the lead, but as dusk approached the officials called him into the pits for adjustments to the rear lights. This took fifteen vital minutes and by the time Taylor was back on the track it was simply impossible for him to make up the time. However, bad luck was to hit Unett again, for the Tiger eventually stopped with a broken rear axle. This was particularly unfortunate, for Bernard had scored the maximum qualifying points for the championship and was robbed of certain victory. By 9.15 pm the race was over. Tony Sergeant was the winner — one of only thirteen track survivors.

In 1966, Bernard Unett was given a second try at the *Autosport* Championship when Alan Fraser invited him to drive a Fraser team car. Fraser was already well known to Rootes' competitions department and had been a good friend of Norman Garrard since 1952. After he had been given the opportunity to drive the Shelby Alpine V8 prototype, Fraser became interested in the Tiger project. In mid-1964 he bought a left-hand drive export car from Rootes (B9470021, reg no 9D). He used this extensively as personal transport on rallies, when organizing his own rally team, and later, during 1965, as a Group 3 car, driven by Andrew Boyd.

Perhaps the most important event in which Fraser entered this Group 3 Tiger was the Ilford Films 500 mile race held at Brands Hatch in May 1966. Driven by Bernard Unett and Ray Calcutt (one of Fraser's most successful Imp drivers) the Tiger faced an impressive line-up: a 7-litre Cobra (Piper/Bondurant), a 4.7-litre Cobra (Pike/Irwin), and a Ferrari 250LM (Salmon/Hobbs), to name a few, together with the Ford GT40s, E-type Jaguars and Lotus Elans. It was an exciting race, many cars being forced to stop because of the rain or various malfunctions. After four hours, the order was Bondurant, Unett, and Sutcliffe in a GT40. With half an hour to go, on lap 168, Unett retired with a broken wheel bearing, but had at least shown that the Tiger could be a competitive car in the right hands. The race was won by a Cobra with an MGB in second place.

In January 1966, Alan Fraser and Geoffrey Rootes signed an agreement concerning the involvement of Team Fraser Imps in international events. However, in order that his drivers and mechanics should get the maximum experience, Fraser decided to enter his cars in national events as well, and to develop a Tiger for the specific purpose of entering it in the *Autosport* Championship.

For this, a new 'marque', known as the 'Monster' Tiger was built, using some of the parts from Unett's original Le Mans racer. A standard production car

Bernard Unett driving the Group 3 Fraser Tiger in the Brands Hatch 500, early May 1965. (Photo: Motorsport)

body was stripped down and strengthened, the suspension being carried by additional brackets. After the car had been lowered by approximately 2½ inches, competition specification coil springs were fitted along with Armstrong adjustable dampers. The 4.7:1 rear axle, complete with parallel links, and the gearbox were transferred from Unett's old car. The 4.2-litre engine was prepared by Fraser's engineers using a 260 block fitted with Cobra-type 289 cylinder heads and crankshaft. The whole engine was balanced and four twin-choke 45DCOE Weber carburettors were added, along with a pair of high pressure SU petrol

A BARC club meeting at Silverstone, early October 1966. (Photo: Motorsport)

pumps. The result was an engine which produced approximately 300-325 bhp. With its alloy bonnet, boot-lid and hardtop, the car tipped the scales at 2464 lbs with 10 gallons of fuel.

In early October, the final of the Freddie Dixon Trophy was held at Silverstone. Unett found himself up against an old rival, Warren Pearce in a 3.8-litre Jaguar E-type. To gain the trophy he had to win the race outright. However, another old adversary, Tommy Entwistle in his TVR 1800S, had to achieve only third place to secure the Championship. From the start to the last lap of the race Pearce tailed Unett. Then Pearce made a desperate attempt to overtake at Woodcote. His E-type easily outbraked the Tiger, but went wide. Unett took the advantage and burst ahead. Pearce recovered and gradually gained ground until only inches separated them as they passed the finishing line. Entwistle came in an easy third, thereby taking the trophy. Unett was second overall, but first in his class.

Later in the month, the *Autosport* Championship was held at Snetterton. With excellent timing and good co-operation, Unett achieved the impossible by practising and racing in two events in one day. After a resounding victory at Brands Hatch, a private plane flew him up to Snetterton to drive the Tiger. This was the one big event of the day in which Unett was to compete against Brian Muir (in an AC Cobra) who was favourite for the trophy.

There was an impressive line-up on the starting grid: Brian Muir (Cobra), Willie Green (Ginetta) and John Miles (Elan) made up the front row. Colin

Crabbe (Aston Martin) and Gerry Marshall (TVR Griffith) were in the second row. Behind them in the third row were Martin Hone (Porsche), Don Marriot (Elan) and Warren Pearce (E-type Jaguar). In the fourth row, after practising on a wet track, was Bernard Unett.

As the flag went down, the Aston of Colin Crabbe refused to start and Unett nipped smartly in front. By the end of the first lap the positions were: Muir, Green, Marshall, Miles, Unett and Pearce. On the second lap Unett overtook John Miles, while the Muir Cobra was hard pressed by the Ginetta of Willie Green, staying in front only with difficulty. Then Unett passed Gerry Marshall and, as the race drew to an end, the leaders started to lap those at the rear. First home was Brian Muir, followed by Willie Green with Bernard Unett in third place. As Miles needed only a second in class, he took the *Autosport* Trophy for 1966 with Bernard Unett second and class winner.

In July 1966, John Blunsden had tested the Alan Fraser 'marque' Tiger for *Motor Racing* at Brands Hatch. Unfortunately, although the car was fitted with the original Le Mans wheels, it did not have its wide section tyres, and this resulted in a light rear end. Inevitably, the tail broke away early, which meant that the car had to be set up well in advance of any approaching corner. All the bends required careful use of power and steering to obtain the best results. Third gear proved excellent for all but the sharpest bends, where second had to be used,

The engine of the Team Fraser race Tiger. No chrome; just plenty of power. (Photo: P. Harper)

One Tiger and two Imps in transport. After Rootes had withdrawn their support from Alan Fraser's racing team, he terminated his business commitments and went to Teneriffe. (Photo: P. Harper)

while the Pit Straight called for a change into top, using 6000 as the rev limit. Blunsden found that the steering was ideal over smooth surfaces, but that any undulations caused a pitching from the suspension which was transmitted from the driver to the steering. Nevertheless, he found the car exciting to drive, while choosing the right line through a bend produced a feeling of great satisfaction. According to Blunsden, the car sounded just marvellous!

In 1967, Alan Fraser was invited by the Rootes concessionaires in Teneriffe to take a team of Imps and Tigers to the fourth Gran Premio de Teneriffe. Peter Harper finished in first place, driving the 'Monster'. This was to be the last time the car was used by Fraser — a fitting finale for the last of the racing Tigers.

The Tiger Stateside

Designed with the US market in mind, the Tiger's performance on American race tracks was obviously a significant factor when it came to selling cars in the showrooms. The responsibility for organizing the Tiger's racing career in the States lay primarily with John Panks, based in New York, and with Ian Garrad in California.

John Panks returned to Britain in 1965 after spending twenty-one years in North America. During this time, he became Director of Rootes Motors Inc, the American-based company which handled Rootes' interests in the United States and Canada. 'By the end of that time,' Panks recalls, 'I had become an American. I thought like one and acted like one.'

His successor was Malcolm Freshney, who had previously been in charge of Rootes' interests in Canada. As soon as he had taken over, Freshney set about organizing a survey of Rootes Motors Inc's distributor network in the States. It took three to four months to complete and, with certain amendments, was accepted by Rootes in the UK. However, Freshney had only just embarked upon implementing his rearrangements when a telex arrived from Coventry, saying 'Stop all rearrangement proceedings'. It just happened that Chrysler's chairman had been present at the board meeting during which Freshney's proposals were approved. As a result, he gave instructions for the gradual run-down of Rootes' distributors in the States, a job Freshney found 'soul destroying'.

Ian Garrad moved to North America in 1951. By 1965, he had risen to become

Malcolm Freshney introducing the Sunbeam Tiger on Canadian television. (Photo: Chrysler UK)

Rootes Motors Inc's West Coast manager. He was a shrewd judge of the American automobile market, and was astute enough to realize that when it came to selling sports cars, several wins on the race track were worth more than a concentrated advertising campaign. In order to promote the good name of Rootes, and Sunbeam in particular, he went out of his way to encourage and support those West Coast drivers who drove Alpines in local events.

Remote from the Rootes factory, Garrad was not in a strong position to make any appeal for a more powerful version of the Alpine. Even Panks (whose offices were situated in New York) often felt like a voice in the wilderness. In the absence of any directive from Rootes, Garrad decided to act independently. As already described, he arranged for two prototype cars to be built, constructed around Rootes bodies and fitted with Ford V8 engines. A demonstration of one of these cars was sufficient to convince Lord Rootes of the car's capability, and the Sunbeam Tiger was born. It was shown for the first time at the New York Motor Show in April 1964, where Brian Rootes commented that 'The production and development of this car has been a team effort on both sides of the Atlantic, and the combination of the basic Sunbeam Alpine design and the lightweight Ford engine has proved brilliantly successful.

'By using thoroughly proved components, we have been able to achieve a very competitive price and we are confident that this additional high-performance model, together with the $1\frac{1}{2}$-litre Alpine, will help us to considerably increase our volume of sports car sales in the US.'

As with the Alpine, Garrad sought to promote the new sports car through publicity from racing. To the buying public, it was crucial that the Alpine V8 should be seen to perform well in competition and not just look the part. Prospective customers needed to associate the car with a reputation, a reputation built on success. Clearly, it was imperative that Rootes Motors Inc became directly involved with motor racing. As John Panks explained: 'Racing in America is a national scene, so we encouraged dealer participation in local events — the financial backing for our competition programme coming from the Rootes Motors Inc budget.'

To Garrad, this was a step in the right direction, but not enough. He had nothing less than a comprehensive race programme in mind, and with Pank's approval he now set about organizing the construction of a Tiger especially suited to national events. As Shelby had built the white demonstration Alpine V8, Garrad suggested that he might like to construct a race car suitable for Class 'B' production races. The enterprising Shelby agreed. In early March, 1964, the prototype vehicle AF3 was flown over from Coventry to Shelby's workshop in California where a tuned 260 cu in (4.2 litre) engine was installed. Modifications were made to the suspension and the entire bodywork was resprayed yellow. When the work had been completed, Ken Miles took the car to Riverside Raceway for handling evaluation. Although Shelby had amassed a team of highly skilled engineers, during this period they were all heavily involved with other projects. This precluded the team from spending enough time on developing the race Tiger, and much to Shelby's chagrin, this was to be only too evident in subsequent races.

The car was to race in Class 'B' events against such vehicles as 'older' Corvettes and six cylinder E-type Jaguars. Its first outing was to Tucson, Arizona for the Pacific Coast Divisional Championships. Driven by Lew Spencer, it was unsuccessful but, as one reporter noted, it looked promising. Later, in the Pacific Coast Divisional Championships at Willow Springs, Lew Spencer made history

Lew Spencer at the wheel of the Shelby-built racing Tiger at Willow Springs. He finished first in the B production event. (Photo: Autocar)

The interior of the engine compartment, showing the race prepared 260 cu in Tiger power unit. (Photo: D. Spencer)

by being the first man to win a race in a Sunbeam Tiger, finishing 12 seconds in front of his nearest rival who was driving an E-type Jaguar. In September of the same year, Lew drove the Tiger in the 200 mile National Sports Car Race at Elkhart Lake, where he finished second overall and first in class. Lew Spencer recalls, 'Apart from the cooling problems, the Tiger was always a little frightening to drive on a race track because of its short wheelbase.'

Despite Lew's performance at Willow Springs and Elkhart Lake, 1964 proved highly unsuccessful for the Shelby Tiger as a race car. At both the Laguna Seca and Kent (Washington) race tracks the car crashed because of its poor handling. This disappointing record depressed Garrad and he decided to approach Doane Spencer of Hollywood Sports Cars, to ask him if he would develop another race Tiger for the 1965 season. Hollywood Sports Cars had held an MG franchise for some years, and Doane had been responsible for preparing their race cars — which were very successful. He had also been involved with the Shelby Alpine V8 prototype. His experience was the envy of many in the motor racing world. Doane agreed to take on the project, and in late 1964 a light blue Tiger was delivered to the Hollywood workshop. This car had been a Rootes Motors Inc demonstration vehicle and had only a few miles on the hodometer. Doane's solu-

The rear of the Spencer-built Hollywood Sports Cars race Tiger. With the wheel removed, the disc brake is clearly visible as is the aluminium panel behind the driver's seat. Note also the modified windscreen. (Photo: D. Spencer)

tion to the Tiger's overheating problems was to clear the engine compartment of all ancillaries. Parts such as the brake servo were repositioned under the front wings. Reverse louvres in the bonnet and ducts cut in the wings (similar to those on the British rally cars) helped to channel away the heat from inside the engine compartment. Like the Coventry engineers, Doane realized that the hot air which gathered under the bonnet had to be freed. In addition, a radiator with thicker cores was installed, but here, Doane was careful to ensure that the stock top and bottom tanks were retained, 'so that it looked standard'.

Doane used cast alloy wheels with a 7 inch rim width and designed a new differential casing which allowed for a greater quantity of oil. Girling disc brake assemblies, similar to those used on Daimlers (Doane's description), were obtained from a local supplier and fitted in place of the rear drum set-up. In some cases, Austin Healey parts were used on the suspension where Doane considered them to be superior to the Rootes components.

When the car was finished it was taken to Willow Springs race track for testing and evaluation. The engine produced 349 bhp — which was subsequently found powerful enough to lift the front wheels fractionally on a change up to top gear

Doane Spencer testing out the position of the driving seat. His wealth of experience in the motor racing world was reflected dramatically in the performance of this car. (Photo: D. Spencer)

along the straight at Santa Barbara! Garrad was extremely pleased with the result.

Rootes had invested nearly $40,000 in this race Tiger and were naturally anxious to see how the car would perform. Its first outing was at the Santa Barbara Road Races in late May 1965. Resplendent in its new black livery and with the number '55' clearly visible on doors and bonnet, Jim Adams finished first in the Class 'B' production event. This was a very gratifying result, both for Garrad and for Spencer, who had worked hard to ensure the car's success.

Not unnaturally, the car suffered some teething troubles in its early days. The steering proved to be too 'slow' for racing purposes, as Jim Adams discovered to his cost when practising at Candlestick Park, San Francisco. The track bar bent on full lock, thus preventing the wheels from self-centring and leaving Adams no alternative but to withdraw from the race. This was a pity, for Adams had tied with Phil Hill for the fastest qualifying lap time. (Although it was only an amateur event, Ford had decided to use the meeting for a concentrated advertising campaign, which was why Phil Hill was present, driving Ken Miles's 427 Cobra). In the words of Doane Spencer, 'Candlestick Park is a thrilling track and Adams had done very well, but there was nothing for it but to pack up and go home.' This experience spurred Doane into making up a new steering rack mechanism, which he fitted into the standard housing. He also altered the front

Adams going into high gear at Santa Barbara, the front wheels almost lifting off the ground. (Photo: D. Spencer)

brake caliper arrangement to allow for straight track rods. Doane estimated that the Tiger was 'approximately 9 to 11 seconds slower on any given circuit than the current Chaparral — which gives an indication of how competitive we were.'

The full race programme Garrad had drawn up demanded a tight time schedule. The car was flown the 3000 miles to Ontario, Canada for the Mosport 200 race meeting at Mosport Park, where a crowd of 60,000 cheered Adams home after he had led the 15 lap Production Sports Car Race from start to finish.

The following week, Adams and the team were back in California. On 12 June, he won the 'B' Class production event at the Stockton Road Races, making it the third win in three weeks! As one motoring correspondent noted, 'A good car, well driven.'

On 11 July, Adams was at Salt Lake City for the Utah National Points Race where he won his class again. The following month, at the Saint Louis Obispo Road Races, Adams realized his greatest triumph. Against formidable opposition

Telefax

WESTERN UNION

SENDING BLANK

CALL LETTERS QCK INTL CHARGE TO ~~ROOTES MOTORS INC JUNE 5/65~~

ROOTESMOTI LONDON ENGLAND

SUNBEAM TIGER OUTRIGHT WINNER 15 LAP FEATURE RACE FOR PRODUCTION SPORTS CARS AT PLAYERS 200 EVENT MOSPORT ONTARIO CANADA STOP SECOND PLACE 8 SECONDS BEHIND WAS SHELBY MUSTANG 350 THIRD SHELBY COBRA FOURTH PORSCHE STOP CHEERING CROWD IN EXCESS OF 60,000 SAW TIGER LEAD FROM START TO FINISH STOP CAR PREPARED BY HOLLYWOOD SPORTS CARS HOLLYWOOD CALIFORNIA AND FLOWN 3000 MILES TO MOSPORT BY FLYING TIGER AIRLINE TO RACE STOP DRIVER JIM ADAMS STOP MECHANIC DOANE SPENCER STOP THIS IS MOST IMPORTANT RACE ON CANADIAN CALENDAR.

GARRAD

Send the above message, subject to the terms on back hereof, which are hereby agreed to

PLEASE TYPE OR WRITE PLAINLY WITHIN BORDER—DO NOT FOLD

Copy of a jubilant telex message sent by Garrad to Rootes, Coventry.

Jim Adams dogging the Cobra at Stockton Raceway, California. He used no brakes, because the temperature was so high and the course so tight, until the last corner, when he went under the Cobra to win. (Photo: D. Spencer)

John Drew's immaculate Mk II Tiger, originally owned by Alan Hartwell.

Thrilling new high performance, in a luxury sports tourer! A new Sunbeam Alpine V8, with more power and speed, more powerful acceleration, new engine features and exclusive styling refinements. Plus all the renowned Alpine features—superb road-holding, ease of handling, luxury comfort and safety!

For sheer pleasure, try the exciting new Mark II. The unique lightweight V8 engine now has capacity increased to 4,737 c.c. You enjoy quiet, flexible performance and smooth operation with the thrill of V8 punch and power. You get instant throttle response, vivid acceleration in all gears, sustained cruising speeds of 115 m.p.h. (185 k.p.h.), and a top speed of 125 m.p.h. (200 k.p.h.). With lusty power for hill and mountain climbs—and fuel economy.

Sunbeam Alpine V8 is a great car in traffic, too. Easy to handle and control, docile. You can loiter in top at 20 m.p.h. (32 k.p.h.), or crawl to a standstill in second. Then, you're off in a flash, with lightning acceleration—from 0-60 m.p.h. (0-96 k.p.h.) in 7.8 seconds!

The safety of Alpine's brilliant design has been fully proved in numerous sporting successes. An advanced suspension system and balanced weight distribution give tenacious road-hold. Braking is smooth and powerful. Controls are light and precise—the control panel and driving position were designed by racing experts. Tough, all-steel unitary contruction ensures all-round protection. Last—but not least—you have the reliability of Sunbeam fine engineering and quality!

Adams coming in first overall at Willow Springs, California. (Photo: D. Spencer)

Doane Spencer's wife and daughter, Wendy, taking the victory lap after the Tiger's first overall win, at Willow Springs, California. (Photo: D. Spencer)

he had an outright win, proving beyond all doubt the capabilities of the Tiger.

At the Riverside Raceway, '55' was timed at 160 mph. In some people's opinion, the car was always a little 'twitchy' but this was more than compensated for by its straight line performance. At the Pacific Coast Divisional Championships, Adams finished third behind Jerry Titus in the 'B' production champion's Shelby GT-350 and Merle Brenen in the National Kingpin E-type Jaguar.

In mid-1965, Jim Adams broke his leg and was thus prevented from driving in subsequent race meetings. Garrad, anxious to keep the car on the tracks, was all for letting someone else drive, but Doane was reluctant because of the 'illegal' modifications he had made to the Tiger — in particular, its quicker steering. He thus made sure that it was never in a fit state to race, until Adams was able to drive again. In fact, Doane was quite confident that they would still win the season in view of the points they had accumulated so far. Unfortunately, his confidence was short-lived. The last race of the season, the American Road Race of Champions, was to be held at Daytona and Adams, his leg still in plaster, was to drive the Tiger for the first time since his accident. His practice time earned him a good place on the grid, outqualifying everything but a 427 Cobra and two Shelby GT350s. But then, during the first lap of the race itself, on a part of the circuit where the leaders loop back on the tail-enders, a 427 Corvette from the rear of the grid swerved across the grass, only to crash into Adams, hitting the Tiger in the rear and moving the suspension over by nearly 6 inches. Adams was out of the race and Garrard was furious!

Doane offered to take the Tiger home and rebuild it if Garrad supplied the parts, but Garrad refused. It is possible that the racing budget assigned for 1965 had been spent. However, Garrad was offered $5000 for the car, which he accepted. Before it was taken away, Doane was careful to remove the final drive assembly, pistons and cylinder head which were his property, replacing them with standard components. In his words, 'I didn't want to show all those dummies how to set up a 260 engine.'

As the season had begun so well for Doane and Jim, Daytona was a bitter disappointment. But their efforts were not entirely in vain. For news of the early performances of the Hollywood Sports Cars' Tiger had reached Rootes in Coventry, and in particular the Rootes development engineers. They were impressed by what they had heard and wanted to learn the secrets behind the car's successes. They were especially intrigued by Doane's cure for the overheating problem, not to mention his ability to get the car to handle satisfactorily on a race track. In order to see these modifications at first hand, and to to discuss them with Doane Spencer, in September 1965 Alec Caine went to Los Angeles. The purpose of the meeting was to evaluate the alterations and assess their merits, with a view to their possible incorporation in production models. Here are some of the points which were raised.

The 14 inch diameter Mustang wheels could be adopted for the Tiger. With improved brake cooling, these would allow for the use of larger diameter discs. Doane had experienced problems with the front calipers under race conditions and had had to take steps to overcome distortion. He had fitted Daimler Girling rear disc brakes in conjunction with a special valve which altered the pressure proportion between the front and rear brakes. The valve could be obtained either in fixed ratio or fully adjustable.

The front disc brake assembly had been reversed on the stub axle carrier. This modification allowed straight track rods to be used which consequently reduced the reverse Ackerman effect. This, in turn, made it possible to use a steering rack with a higher (quicker) ratio. For the future, Doane had intended to modify the front crossmember which would in effect have buried the steering rack.

Doane had overcome rear spring wind-up under heavy acceleration by removing the metacentric bush and fitting an additional half spring (from the axle forward) clipped at each main spring leaf.

As the rear axle assembly on the standard Tiger was too heavy for racing, Doane had substituted a type 23 'Dana' axle with Hi-nickel shafts which was considerably lighter. The limited-slip differential also displaced a large quantity of oil in the standard casing, and so Doane had fabricated an aluminium casing allowing for a greater quantity of oil.

For racing, engine cooling was of primary importance and Doane had fitted a larger radiator. To assist the through flow of air under the bonnet, he had moved the header tank and dynamo, and cut holes in the rear of the front wings (fenders) with ducting attached to channel the air away.

It can be assumed that the work and opinions of Doane Spencer must have been held in high regard for Rootes to send one of their senior project engineers to Hollywood. Certainly, the trip was beneficial to both men. Doane well remembers how Alec was able to help him over certain points on carburation while Alec, on his return to Coventry, usefully employed the information he had acquired from Doane when he started to develop the all disc braked Tiger.

While much of the limelight was inevitably captured by '55', other racing Tigers were also successful in the States during 1965. A Tiger driven by Peter Boulton and John Latta finished twelfth overall and first in the 'Small Bore' GT class in the Daytona Continental, and in Danville, Virginia, Don Sesslar finished first in the 'B' class production and second overall in the Danville National Races in April. It was Sesslar, too, who held the lap speed record at the Mid Ohio Raceway for 'A' and 'B' production cars.

In 1966, the racing Tigers were not so successful. The Hollywood Sports Car Tiger was now in the hands of Ron Dykes, sponsored by Vincent Motors. Its only notable outing was at the Los Angeles GP at Riverside Raceway in October. There the car finished fourth overall in the combined 'A' and 'B' class production race and won its own 'B' Class production event in full view of 80,000 spectators. It reached speeds of up to 157 mph along the straight where its acceleration proved too much for the opposition.

In 1967, drastic alterations were made to the regulations governing production events, with far reaching effects on the Tiger's racing career. The Sports Car Club of America reclassified the Tiger into 'C' Class production with the result that it became virtually uncompetitive overnight. Under its new racing category, all the worth-while modifications and LAT options (performance accessories available from Rootes Motors Inc) were forbidden. Items such as high-rise manifolds, four-barrel Holley carburettors, 13 x 7 inch wheels and Ford Hi Po dual point distributor (which were vital to the Tiger's competitiveness) were

After Jim Adams's crash at Daytona, Garrad sold the Hollywood Sports Cars Tiger. Here, Ron Dykes lines up on the grid at Riverside Raceway, California. (Photo: I. Garrad)

Against formidable opposition, Dykes still managed to show the spectators how well the Tiger could perform, winning the Class B Production race. (Photo: I. Garrad)

withdrawn. Under its 'C' production classification, the Tiger had to race with a two barrel carburettor, a cast iron manifold, and a maximum wheel rim width of 6 inches. Against such cars as Triumph and Porsche, the Tiger was just no match.

In 1975, Dave Johnson of White Tiger Racing (Milwaukee) wrote to the SCCA with a convincing argument for altering the regulations affecting the Tiger (though it was clearly far too late to make any appreciable difference). His suggestions included: the use of a four-barrel Holley carburettor, an increase of 2 inches all round in the track, and an increase in the wheel rim width listing from 13 x $4\frac{1}{2}$ to 13 x $6\frac{1}{2}$ inches, which would allow the Tiger a maximum wheel width of 13 x 8 inches — as the SCCA permitted an extra $1\frac{1}{2}$ inches above the standard listing for production specification.

Unfortunately, while the preceding points were accepted, Johnson's request for alterations to the Tiger's power unit were rejected. He had suggested the inclusion of the 302 cu in (5.4-litre) cylinder block, crankshaft, connecting rods, and cylinder head because of the increasing difficulty in obtaining parts for the 260 and 289 cu in engines.

For two consecutive years, in 1974 and 1975, a Tiger won the SCCA Solo 2 'B' prepared class National Championship — an indication of just how effective the car could be, when the rules covering updating were commensurate with the availability of spares.

But track racing was not the only type of event to capture the imagination of the enterprising Garrad. Although John Panks is adamant that 'this was not the type of image we were trying to create for the Tiger', another competition car with which Rootes Motors Inc became involved was the Larry Reed sponsored Tigers, developed for American Hot Rod Association events. Such men as Cliff

The factory-entered Tiger of Larry Reed Sports Cars. This car was driven by Gordon Chittenden, who later wrote a book, Performance Tuning the Sunbeam Tiger. (Photo: I. Garrad)

Dave Johnson and White Tiger Racing's Sunbeam Tiger at Indianapolis Park, 1976. (Photo: D. Johnson)

RACING

Stan Peterson's Class C Tiger winning the Stock National Hot Rod Association Championship at Vacca Valley, California, in May 1965. It reached 110 mph in the standing quarter mile in 12.95 seconds. (Photo: Chrysler UK)

Brien, Wally Cartwright, Danny Shields, Don Von, Bill Woodul and Ron Root all helped to produce this very potent machine. Driven by Gordon Chittenden, the car was the National Record Holder in the AHRA in 1965, 1966 and 1967, covering the standing start $\frac{1}{4}$ mile in 12.95 seconds with a terminal speed of 108 mph. Chittenden wrote a book, *Performance Tuning the Sunbeam Tiger,* in which he described the modifications made to his car and outlined the possible alterations which could be made by the average owner.

In May 1965 Stan Peterson's 'C' stock Tiger won the National Hot Rod Association World Championship at Vacca Valley. It covered the standing start $\frac{1}{4}$ mile in 12.9 seconds with a terminal speed of 110 mph. Of the two associations, the NHRA is the larger and is more stringent in its competition preparation regulations.

The competition successes of all these Tigers, especially during 1965, produced excellent publicity, which in turn was of direct benefit to Rootes' sales effort. In addition, competitive events formed ideal test beds for the development of a range of performance options which were marketed specifically for the Sunbeam Tiger. The bolt-on accessory market was already a thriving business, and Rootes Motors Inc were anxious to cash in on this lucrative side-line. Known as LAT options (after the IBM computer stock control print-out), these were introduced in

Art Arfons reflects on the Tiger after making several high speed runs around Riverside Raceway. A subsequent trip to Los Angeles and back netted him three speeding offences. (Photo: I. Garrad)

1965 and produced in conjunction with Hollywood Sports Cars. They were available from the Rootes Motors Inc parts department, customers outside America being obliged to order by post. (Rootes' competitions department in Coventry offered its own list of performance parts, which could be obtained through Rootes dealers, although the range was not nearly as comprehensive.)

It was during the construction of the Hollywood Sports Cars' race Tiger that the LAT options were designed and developed. Doane Spencer supplied the drawings from which Roland Soll, another member of the team, made the patterns. Accessories such as differentials and manifolds were designed and prototypes made for evaluation. The first batch of alloy wheels suffered from structural weaknesses and Spencer ultimately sought an alternative foundry to cast stronger wheels. As Spencer remembers, 'All the options had to be of a universal fitting so that they could be installed on any standard Tiger, otherwise they infringed the regulations.' Those options listed in the homologation papers had to be submitted to the SCCA and the FIA for approval. In addition, Garrad and his parts manager, Richard Wheatley, had to ensure that all the listed options were carried by their stores and available from stock. Inevitably, this included the more sophisticated items such as hand-made, long-range fuel tanks. With such a quantity of stock, the store's value was constantly in the region of $40,000.

In addition to the LAT performance options, there was a range of approved accessories which could also be installed to special order:

1. Long-range fuel tank and special fuel pump.
2. Rear disc brakes.
3. Engine compartment air outlets for the front wings.
4. Lightweight aluminium extra capacity radiator.
5. Wing flares to accommodate oversize tyres.

When a car was ordered with LAT options, the work was carried out at either the Rootes Motors Inc warehouses at Long Beach, California, or at Long Island City, New York.

Unfortunately, from the outset there were difficulties with these LAT modifications. Garrad was often criticized for the alterations which were made to Jim Adams's racing Tiger, although there was no doubt that the car (from the outside at least) complied with the regulations. For SCCA Solo 2 events, the specifications were clear in their requirements. A part was considered 'stock' if: 'an item of standard equipment could have been ordered with the car, installed on the factory production line and delivered through a dealer in the United States. Dealer installed options, no matter how common, are not included in this

Ian Garrad receiving the British Automobile Manufacturers' Award for his outstanding contribution to the British motor car industry. The retail value of Tigers and parts sold was approximately $28 million. (Photo: I. Garrad)

definition.' The problem arose over the location of the factory and the dealer chain. Clearly, the factory production line was Jensen Motors at West Bromwich, but as the options were installed before delivery to the dealers, the regulations were not contravened.

None the less important to the Tiger was the excellent publicity it gained through a very different type of competition, for in 1965 and 1966 it won the 'Best Grand Touring Car $2500-3500' award organized by *Car and Driver* magazine. In 1965 the magazine noted that 'the Tiger symbolizes the trend towards a faster, more comfortable medium priced sports car.' The following year it commented that 'the V8 engine turns the otherwise average English sports car into a genuinely exciting vehicle.' 'The Tiger', it said, 'has a tautness missing in many sports cars of its size — the Tiger's here to stay.' How wrong they were.

In America, dealers had little difficulty in selling the Tiger. Hollywood Sports Cars, for example, always had a waiting list of customers. In a very short time, the car had gained immense popularity, a fact which must be almost wholly attributed to the publicity gained from good road test reports, and the efforts made by Rootes Motors Inc in ensuring that it received maximum media exposure.

Unlike the Cobra, the Tiger never enjoyed the extra advantage of intensive

Malcolm Freshney — managing director of Rootes Motors Inc, Ian Garrad and Carroll Shelby admire the Car and Driver *Readers' Choice award. The Tiger received more votes than any other car in the history of the award. It won the following year, too!* (Photo: Ian Garrad)

Rootes Motors Inc were always quick to grab any opportunity to publicize the Tiger. Here a Tiger is used to give Graham Hill a lap of honour.

advertising through Ford. But then, in 1964, Carroll Shelby had signed a five year contract with Ford which was to keep his business profitable and involve a mutually advantageous marketing and technical liaison.

It seems that most prospective buyers were willing to accept the similarity between the Alpine and the Tiger. (In this respect, Lord Rootes was proved right, and Garrad and Panks wrong.) The price was right, the shape was right, and so was the performance. So what went wrong? Why did production stop?

The End of the Road

Before discussing the Tiger's demise, it is essential to trace the history of Chrysler's activities in Europe. In 1958, Chrysler took two major steps towards establishing themselves in a more competitive position outside North America, as Ford and General Motors had done already. The first move was the development of a wholly owned Swiss subsidiary based in Geneva. Known as Chrysler International SA, it was established for the co-ordination and development of the company's overseas marketing and manufacturing organizations. The second move was to invest in the fourth largest motor manufacturer in France, Simca, in which they acquired a quarter of the shares. By 1964, this was increased to 64 per cent, and the company was split in two, one responsible for the manufacture of lorries and tractors and the other for car production.

Chrysler's first links with Rootes came during 1964, when it acquired 45 per cent of the voting shares and 65 per cent of the non-voting shares. During the years 1965 and 1966, the Rootes Group continued to make steadily mounting losses, culminating in an enormous £10 million deficit in 1966/7. Chrysler's 1964 investment was dwindling rapidly: it was time for action. In January 1967, Chrysler took control by increasing their holding of voting shares to 77.3 per cent. On the death of Lord Rootes in December 1964, his younger brother, Sir Reginald, succeeded him as company chairman. In March 1967, he handed the job over to William's son Geoffrey, the new Lord Rootes. In May, Chrysler appointed Gilbert Hunt as managing director and chief executive officer, and it was he who had the task of resurrecting the Rootes Group.

When Chrysler took over, their evaluation of Rootes' operating techniques and monetary situation revealed that a number of major alterations would be required. Foremost amongst these were the implementation of modern accounting techniques and the reorganization of the Rootes Group dealer network. In addition, Chrysler also decided to purchase the Linwood body factory from Pressed Steel Fisher and retool it. Up until then, Rootes had been forced to buy ready-made bodies from Pressed Steel's Cowley plant, which was owned by BMC, thereby giving away a small percentage of the profit made on each vehicle to a rival manufacturer. This arrangement was quite unacceptable to Chrysler, who were adamant that all subsequent bodies should be built within the Group. Unfortunately, this acquisition precluded any spare capital being chanelled into the development of a sports car. In any case, Chrysler considered that the cost of introducing a new sports car was not economically viable, since a large share of the sports car market was already held by BMC and Triumph.

But that is not to say that Rootes did not try to keep the Tiger in production. Indeed, we can only commiserate with the development team for the fact that their plans failed to materialize.

During the latter part of 1966, Rootes realized that a Mk II Tiger fitted with the 4.7-litre Ford engine could have only a short production life. A more far-sighted approach was required if the Tiger was to remain in long-term production. The obvious answer seemed to be the 4.5-litre Chrysler Valiant unit. As Peter Wilson explained, 'Towards the end of 1966 it was generally accepted that Chrysler would take over the controlling interest in Rootes' operations during the following year, and we realized that the Tiger's Ford engine would inevitably cause an embarrassing situation. So we considered the Valiant engine as an alternative. We thought that as it had nearly the same capacity as the Ford unit, it would almost certainly fit, but despite a considerable amount of time spent on planning, it became obvious that we could not use it. The main problem lay in the position of the distributor. The Ford engine was so perfect for the Tiger because it had narrow cylinder banks and a distributor that was mounted at the front of the engine. The Valiant's distributor was mounted at the back, which meant that when the engine was fitted in the Tiger's engine compartment, the distributor fouled the scuttle. We even considered making a removable plate to allow for access, but eventually had to concede defeat and cancel the project.' Wilson is confident that the Tiger would have found a ready market had production continued with the Valiant engine, but considers that in the long term the car would have needed major re-engineering, possibly along the lines of latter-day, mid-engined cars.

'The whole thing was just beginning to gel and move into high gear', remembers John Panks, 'when production of the Tiger ceased and the export flow stopped. But from the start, in my opinion, the car's one big snag was its similarity to the Alpine. There is no doubt in my mind that the Tiger could have

This Chrysler V8 engine developed 235 bhp at 5200 rpm, with a compressed ratio of 10.5:1 and one four-barrel Holley carburettor. The unit also featured a high lift camshaft and domed pistons. The fan projects unusually far forward for such a compact engine. (Photo: Chrysler Detroit)

stayed in production had it been fitted with the Chrysler engine, but it seemed that Chrysler never wanted to create the same forward-looking image that would appeal to the younger generation. This is borne out by their design trends, which always tend to go in bursts.'

However, the reader is invited to judge this view in the light of Chrysler's contemporary designs. These sketches, part of a set produced by the Chrysler design office in Detroit during 1965/6, were proposals for a replacement for the Tiger. Timothy Rootes showed considerable interest in the project, but although many relevant sketches and full-size layouts were produced, nothing was developed in clay. The designs, based on a Chrysler engine, were sent to Coventry (along with suggested designs for other models) for consideration by the Rootes stylists. Had the project been adopted, arrangements would then have been made for the car to be produced in the United Kingdom.

Variations on a theme. These were the first ideas put forward for updating the Tiger. What would Kenneth Howes say? (Photo: Chrysler Detroit)

SUNBEAM

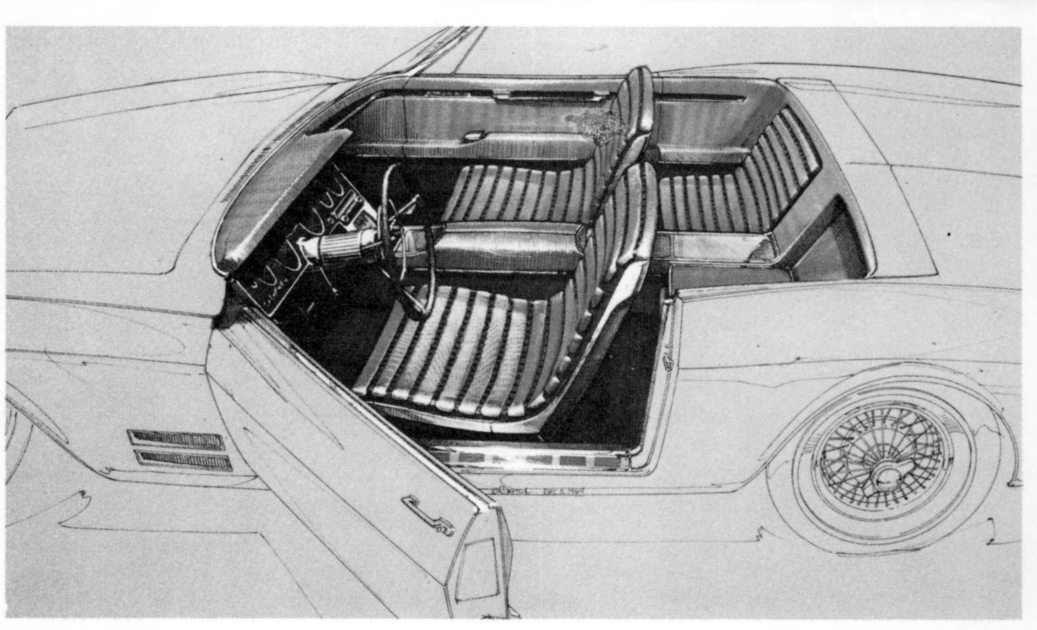

A more radical approach. The hardtop has been fixed and the roofline lowered, while the rear fins have been completely removed. (Photo: Chrysler Detroit)

Opposite:
One possible interior treatment for the new 'Chrysler' Tiger. The angle and layout of the dash are typical of US design of the 1960s. (Photo: Chrysler Detroit)

Several designers in Chrysler's studio in Detroit were asked to give their impressions of an updated Tiger. (Photo: Chrysler Detroit)

The sketches show what the Tiger might have been, had finance allowed. But what of the production Tigers, the cars the Tiger enthusiast has come to know and love?

In recent years the Mk I Tiger has been criticized for its 260 cu in (4.2-litre) engine. Many people feel that the car should have been fitted with the 289 cu in (4.7-litre) unit from the outset, but Lord Rootes had never envisaged a 'Sunbeam Cobra'. Many other questions are asked about the Tiger programme. For example, could the development work have been handled equally well by Rootes themselves without the aid of Jensen? This is certainly unlikely, for at the time Rootes' own development team were heavily committed to the Arrow (Hunter) programme which left little free manpower for taking on extra development work. In addition, the Tiger project demanded skilled engineers familiar with installing large units into small engine compartments. Rootes' engineers, though highly skilled, lacked this essential experience.

As so many Sunbeam Tigers were sold in the States, why did Rootes not send ready-built cars minus engines and transmissions to America in the same way that AC shipped Cobras to Carroll Shelby? It is doubtful whether this was ever considered, for, unlike AC and the Cobra, Rootes envisaged that the Tiger would eventually sell in substantial numbers in Europe as well as in the States. Installing the engines in America would have created a transportation problem, notwithstanding the difficulties of keeping a strict control over the final production quality. However, it is thought that the American West Coast personnel were already to take over production had Rootes in England been agreeable.

Finally, in view of the car's short production run, it is reasonable to ask, was the Tiger a commercial success? The answer must undoubtedly be yes. While it appears that there may have been a degree of hesitation, almost embarrassment, on the part of some salesmen when it came to knowing how to market the car, it would appear that dealers in both Britain and the States had little difficulty in selling the Tiger, and few, if any, were left collecting dust in showrooms.

However, although the Alpine had been in production some five years by the time the Tiger was launched, it had not established the long-standing reputation normally associated with cars such as MG and Austin Healey. The casual buyer just did not expect to see a V8 powered sports car in Rootes' catalogue, and dealers with connections with motor sport sometimes found it easier to sell the Tiger than those who concentrated on saloons. Peter Wilson illustrated this point: 'I remember there were cases where a large Rootes franchise could sell only a couple of Tigers, whereas a much smaller retail dealer with an active interest in motor sport could often sell a dozen or more.'

One of the big stumbling blocks for a potential Tiger customer, especially a young one, was the high insurance rating, despite the car's low state of tune. In some cases sales had to be cancelled because the customer could afford the car but not the insurance.

Alan Hartwell, George Hartwell's son, recalled, 'Invariably, customers for the new Tigers fell into two categories: those who had owned an Alpine and had been perfectly happy with it, and bought a Tiger because they saw it as a more "luxurious" version; and those people who always bought Rootes, and always bought the top of the range. For those people, some of whom were women, the Tiger represented just such a model and therefore an obvious choice. I remember a customer driving into our garage reception and complaining that his Tiger was not running quite right, so our service manager lifted the bonnet only to find that two of the plug leads had fallen off. "Oh well", said the customer, "that still leaves 50 per cent more power than I'm normally used to." '

In addition to selling a considerable number of Mk I Tigers, in mid-1967 Alan Hartwell purchased seven export Mk IIs which had been destined for America but had for some reason been delayed. The 289 cu in (4.7 litre) engines as supplied by Ford complied with the American emission regulations. When Hartwell heard that the cars were standing on the dockside at Southampton, he immediately telephoned Rootes to ask if he could buy them. However, this seemingly simple request was fraught with difficulties, and Hartwell spent a considerable amount of time over negotiations before finally taking delivery. It is possible that Rootes were just not in favour of the deal, although it appears that there was some difficulty in calculating the amount of purchase tax which had to be paid. Only six of the seven cars arrived at Hartwell's Bournemouth garage, as he sold the seventh to a Canadian who took immediate delivery. During the winter of 1967/8, the six cars were converted from left-hand to right-hand drive and Minilite magnesium alloy wheels were fitted.

In the spring, advertisements were placed in the national Press offering five Tigers for sale at £1500 each. It was only necessary to advertise them once, as all five cars were sold immediately. 'My father was very unhappy about the purchase of these Tigers', recalls Alan Hartwell, 'so I wanted to sell them as quickly as possible, but, on reflection, I think I probably sold them too cheaply.' The sixth car (which had a vinyl-covered hardtop) Hartwell kept for his own personal use before selling it with approximately 10,000 miles on the hodometer to a friend of his father.

The Tiger found its niche with the Metropolitan Police Force, taking over from the Daimler SP250 as a high-speed patrol car. These were required for dealing with traffic offences, mainly in connection with infringements of speed limits. Four Mk I Tigers formed part of a larger consignment of Rootes vehicles ordered by the Metropolitan Police and delivered in September 1966. In April 1967 a further six, this time Mk IIs, were bought. All the cars were white and came supplied with hard tops. During their 2-2½ years of service, the cars suffered from seat fractures and clutch troubles, but by far the worst problem was routine servicing — it took 2½ hours to change a set of spark plugs!

In fact, it appears that the Police Mk II Tigers formed part of a small quantity

The first of several Police Sunbeam Tigers. The cars were fitted with Traction Master anti-tramp bars, supplied to Scotland Yard by Rootes Motors Inc.

The two Sunbeam Tigers used by the Leeds Police Force. They were kept for appoximately three years and covered 100,000 miles each. One traffic police officer recalls that 'they were fantastic cars'. (Photo: Autocar)

of right-hand-drive cars (possibly as many as 28) which were built in April 1967. Unfortunately, Chrysler's records are not specific on this point, but what is clear is that those 'in the know' were able to purchase a right-hand-drive Tiger Mk II before production finally returned to left-hand-drive only.

Maurice Smith, editorial director of IPC Transport Press, had the use of two Sunbeam Tigers during his term as editor of *Autocar.* The first was the Rootes road test car which had been featured in *Autocar*'s 1965 road test, and which later became available when Rootes replaced it with a new model. The second was a genuine Mk II (B 382001528) — in fact, one of the five pre-production cars. This particular vehicle was offered to Maurice after Rootes had finished with it as a development car.

'On becoming acquainted with the Tiger,' says Maurice, 'I was agreeably surprised. Although it was a car one always had to watch in wet weather, it was sheer fun as a 'Q' car . . . Both cars were reliable, especially the Mk II, and, with the exception of brake fade on the Mk I, I never experienced any trouble. Some time before the Tiger went out of production, I talked to the Chrysler Company and asked them about their thoughts on the Ford engine. They told me they had no specific feelings whatsoever. Of course, the estimated price of the Mk II car like the one I ran was approximately that of an E-type Jaguar at that time and, clearly, Rootes would have been hard pressed to justify that kind of price for what they were offering.'

There is no doubt that Maurice Smith looks back on his 'Tigering' days with fond memories: 'I thoroughly enjoyed my Tigers. I remember on one occasion, when I was on my way up to Raymond Mays, I had left the motorway and joined the back roads when I met up with an early Porsche Carrera. The Porsche was going very quickly and on the corners he was much faster, but on the straights, between 40 and 100 mph, I could catch him. The Tiger was no mean contender when you wanted to have a go.'

Another motoring magazine editor and Tiger fanatic was the late Gregor Grant of *Autosport.* Like Maurice Smith, he was an enthusiastic owner, appreciating the ease with which the Tiger could cover long distances with such little fuss or mechanical failure. He, too, ran a Mk I car followed by a Mk II.

When reflecting on the Tiger programme, it is easy to conclude that the whole idea was conceived at the wrong time. After all, what future could the car have with Rootes in such weak financial shape and about to be taken over by an American giant?

However, had the plans of Peter Ware (Rootes' engineering director) come to fruition, Rootes' future might well have been very different. It appears that after a visit to the Peugeot factory he became interested in the idea of a Rootes/Peugeot merger, and outlined his plans to Reginald Rootes on his return to Coventry. 'But Reggie wouldn't hear of it,' recalled Peter Ware, 'so the whole thing was dropped.' It is ironic that more than fifteen years later the

A Mk II Tiger originally owned by Gregor Grant. The engine features a Holley carburettor, twin point distributor and high lift cam. (Photo: J. Day)

situation should be reversed. With the Citroen/Peugeot takeover, the future of Chrysler UK and Rootes will no doubt be drastically altered with the rationalization and amalgamation of models.

The Sunbeam Tiger has generated an increasingly enthusiastic following. What, then, is the nature of this fascination for what is, after all, simply an Alpine with a V8 engine?

Clearly, the Tiger's shape and style have passed the test of time, for the car has earned its place in the stable of classic sports cars. Perhaps the key to the question is that to own a Tiger is to identify with a different, albeit recent, era. The Tiger embodies the exuberance and confidence of the 1960s — when cars were fun, when petrol was plentiful and cheap, and when enthusiasm, enterprise and originality were permitted a fuller expression.

It is interesting to observe the strength of identification and respect among owners towards a car which, though developed by a try-and-see technique, nevertheless resulted in a production car reflecting the highest professional standards. Most owners agree that the standard of workmanship is extremely high, and reliability is a celebrated feature. Here, perhaps, we come very close to understanding the mystique of the car.

The Tiger remains an epitaph to the people who were involved with it — individuals rather than committees. Maurice Smith once called the car 'under-rated', but it was only under-rated by those who had never owned or driven one.

Cars, Clubs and Spares

Finally, what of the Tiger twelve years after production ceased? What is it like to buy and run one today? It must be said that purchasing a classic or collector's car such as the Tiger can often be a most frustrating and time-consuming business. Hours spent on journeying to view what has been described as a model in pristine condition will often end only in disappointment. However, in most cases it is just a matter of time and perseverance before the right car is found. Of course, the Tiger clubs can be of enormous help in this respect, for a car bought from a Tiger club member will invariably be a car well looked after.

One factor which simplifies the purchase of a Tiger is that there are only the two Mks to choose between. Again, the total production period was so short that there is little difference between individual cars, be they 1964, 65, 66 or 67 models, except that the later cars will be equipped with the larger engine. This in turn helps the spares situation in that it reduces the numbers of variations of parts, such as clutches, wheel bearings, etc, peculiar to the Tiger.

Although accurate records are not available, it is thought that approximately 28 or so Mk II Tigers were sold in the UK, making them true collector's items in this country. These cars had the larger 289 cu in (4.7-litre) engine fitted complete with HEHB gearbox with wider ratios. Although it would not be true to say that it is impossible to buy one of these cars, the likelihood of finding one advertised in the usual motoring magazines is somewhat slim. However, there are 4.7-litre Tigers to be had, these being Mk I cars which have had the larger engine installed some time after leaving the factory. Obviously, to the purist these cars violate the originality code, but for the enthusiast who is just looking for extra performance, a Tiger Mk I with a 289 cu in engine is the answer.

As with the majority of classic cars (or, for that matter, any elderly vehicle) it is the Tiger's bodywork that brings about its ultimate downfall. For while it is possible to replace worn mechanical components, body panels for most classics, and the Tiger in particular, are scarce and expensive. Some clubs, especially in America, are beginning to have certain panels and even rubber mouldings remade by suitable manufacturers, which has helped to ease the problem enormously.

When surveying a Tiger with a view to purchasing it, much can be gleaned from its general appearance. Its overall outward condition can say a lot for how the car has been treated and how it has withstood the rigours of time. A vendor who has not attempted to clean his car inside or out may well have neglected to service it at regular intervals.

A short road-test of a car such as the Tiger is insufficient. The engine needs to be really warm before an assessment can be made of its true condition. The manufacturers specify an oil pressure of approximately 55psi when hot: anything less and the engine may require some major attention.

Another area which can be assessed while the car is being road-tested is the suspension. Because it is so easy to provoke axle tramp in a Tiger, even unintentionally, rear damper wear can be excessive. In some cases, damage may have occurred: for example, the Panhard rod may have been pulled from its mountings. A favourite modification is to fit either Koni or Armstrong adjustable dampers with an obvious benefit to ride and road-holding. On uneven surfaces the Tiger has a tendency towards excessive feedback through the steering. This is characteristic of the marque, but in the opinion of some owners, fitting a smaller leather or woodrim steering wheel helps to reduce the problem.

As for performance, it is difficult to convey to the inexperienced just how quickly a Tiger in good condition should accelerate. The 'aficionado' with years of experience will be able to tell immediately if the engine is either worn or just 'off tune'. To those fresh to a Tiger but used to highly tuned small engines (Mini Cooper S, Cortina GT, etc) the lower revs and much longer pull in the gears will probably be the most noticeable difference. In addition, the V8 engine has a smoothness in operation which is not often found in smaller in-line four cylinder units.

What of the body itself? In the days when the Tiger was in production, factory-applied rust preventatives had not reached the same high standards that they have achieved in latter years. In practice, this means that the prospective Tiger buyer must expect some degree of rust in the monocoque construction body/chassis: it is just a matter of knowing where to look.

The boot floor and spare wheel recess are very vulnerable areas where water

Mike Major, STOC member of Perry Bar, Birmingham, at work on his pre-production works Mk II. (Photo: R. May)

can lie undetected for long periods. Next come the rear wings, especially along the under-edge behind the wheels. This is a favourite place for shoddy fibre glass repairs, should the unscrupulous get to work. Moving forward, the door sills should be checked, although these can often be made good fairly easily with sills from other models, cutting, moulding and welding them in place. Moving forward again, possibly the most susceptible areas to rust are the front wings. The top edges of the inner wheel arches are particularly vulnerable and the prospective purchaser should bear in mind that repairing these could be a very costly job.

Underneath the car, the advice is simple: if the cruciform bracing (added to the Hillman Husky floorpan to give the Alpine/Tiger body greater strength) is badly rusted, then the car should be left alone. The jacking points are to be found at each end of the car and should be carefully inspected. Of course, one way of checking these is to try jacking the car up. If the jacking points emit ominous creaking sounds or just crumble, leaving the car firmly on the ground, their condition is self-evident!

Inside the car, the carpets should be lifted and the floorpan checked. Of particular note is the modified gearbox/clutch cover which is peculiar to the Tiger. This has a habit of rusting along the welded seam where it mates with the original Alpine floorpan.

It is well to make a detailed inspection of the hardtop if one is offered with the car. These are of steel construction and rust seems to attack the areas surrounding the opening rear quarter light. The sealing rubbers should also be examined as these keep the car draught-proof when the hardtop is fitted and cut down irritating wind roar at high speeds. While it is obviously possible to replace the hardtop, it may be difficult to find one in good condition, and even then the colour may not match.

Perhaps one of the first steps to take when purchasing a Sunbeam Tiger is to enrol in one of the Tiger owners' clubs. Membership is essential for any owner, whether he intends to undertake a restoration project, enter for competitions such as autocross or drag racing, or just maintain the car in 'original' condition.

In Great Britain, the Sunbeam Tiger Owners Club, STOC, has an enthusiastic membership of nearly 200. STOC was founded by Andy Bouton and Bill Lynch who, as Tiger fanatics, wanted to meet other owners with similar interests. After discussing how best to launch the club, Andy and Bill placed an advertisement in a national motoring magazine asking all those who were interested to write for further details. Within a matter of months they had sufficient members to organize a meeting, which took place on 27/28 September 1975. Held at Northampton, it was a great success. Since then the club has grown enormously and now holds regional meetings, which eases the burden for those members who do not live in the Home Counties.

STOC member Ken Hubbard sprinting his works experimental 4.7 (AF 204) on the Curborough circuit near Lichfield. (Photo: Ken Hubbard)

The engine compartment of Frank Dryden's 1966 Tiger. The engine is a 'Boss' 302 cu in, with a Holley 850 carburettor, dual point distributor and 3-inch exhaust pipes!

At the Annual General Meeting held in December 1976, a full committee was voted in, consisting of Andy Bouton as chairman, Bill Lynch as secretary, Ray Martin as magazine editor, Dave Woolf as membership secretary (this post has now been taken over by Sally Martin), Chris Beech as public relations officer, and Mike Major as special events and meetings secretary. When the committee was formed, one of the responsibilities of the chairman was that of the spares fund. This was set up so that the club would be able to purchase quantities of spare parts as and when they became available and store them for resale to individual members. This responsibility has now been taken over by a separate committee member, John Drew, whose job it is to carry out this very vital aspect of the club's activities.

Understandably, the largest number of Sunbeam Tiger clubs is in America. In addition to those clubs which deal specifically with the Tiger, other societies cover several marques, one of the more celebrated being the Shelby American Automobile Club which has a membership of over 5500.

One of the first Sunbeam Tiger clubs to be formed in the States was the

No, not the 1964 Le Mans but Silverstone in 1978. The second Le Mans Tiger is competing in the HSCC Group 2 event. (Photo: R. May)

KENNING
Tricentrol
PH

Sunbeam Tiger Owner's Association, STOA, which was started in 1969. Located in San Francisco, it was originally named the Bay Area Sunbeam Tiger Association. Its founders were made up almost entirely from enthusiasts who were interested in the Tiger and its performance potential. Their aim was to share knowledge and experience to mutual advantage and thereby make the Tiger more competitive, especially in events such as autocross and drag racing.

Within two years the club had amassed a considerable following. In addition to the original nucleus of members whose prime concern was competition, there was an increasing number of enthusiasts whose interests lay outside these boundaries. It became obvious that a reorganization was required, and in 1971 the club changed its name to Sunbeam Tiger Owner's Association, and club activities were expanded to cater for most members' tastes. The reorganization has been a great success, and while the competitive spirit has been maintained by such people as Joe Schmidt, who campaigns his Tiger in autocross events, the association's social activities, as in all Tiger clubs, has a very keen following.

The Colorado Association of Tiger Owners, CATO, was formed in 1974 by Don Perez and Darrel Beachy. Like the founders of STOA, Don and Darrel felt that there was a need to collaborate over Tiger knowledge and experience. However, they were also conscious of the gradual decline in the availability of spares, and as Tiger enthusiasts wanted to form a club so as to be in a much stronger position to obtain parts.

Don and Darrel started by contacting known Tiger owners in their area. By the time they held their first meeting, they had a membership of 15 enthusiasts. Since 1974 this has risen to over 60, and club activities include picnics, rallies and autocrosses in addition to the usual club meetings. To date the high-spot of the club's history was in mid-1978 when it held a Tiger convention at Vail, Colorado, where over 50 owners gathered to share each other's company and hear the guest speaker, Ian Garrad.

Although only two of the ten American Tiger clubs have been highlighted here, I hope that this brief description gives some measure of the enthusiasm of Tiger owners and the scope of the clubs' activities.

When asked why the Tiger was so popular in the United States, one Tiger fanatic commented, 'The Sunbeam Tiger has a certain magnetism which the enthusiast finds irresistible. The car is reliable and represents economic motoring for the owner who covers around 40,000 miles per year, and it gives a good deal of fun and excitement.'

In 1974 'Tigers United 1' was held in Medford, Oregon, with representatives from the Sunbeam Tiger Owner's Association, the Pacific Tiger Club, the California Association of Tiger Owners, and the Canadian Tigers Association. Since then, this annual event has become something of an institution, attracting over 150 Tigers and their owners, demonstrating an undiminishing enthusiasm for the Tiger today.

Bill Schaffer, the winner of the Lord Rootes Trophy at Tigers United IV. With him is Ian Garrad, who presented the award.

On the East coast of Canada, the Canadian Tigers Association Inc is a flourishing and active club, whose members keep in constant touch with their fellow enthusiasts in the States. Over in Toronto, Ontario, the Ontario Sunbeam Tiger Owners Club, OSTOC, provides facilities and activities for Tiger enthusiasts in the area. The club began in 1970, when a group of Tiger owners started having regular meetings to discuss their cars and benefit from each other's knowledge. As soon as it became clear that there were sufficient people interested in forming a club, a letter was draughted to Chrysler UK Ltd asking for permission to use the title 'Sunbeam Tiger'. With permission received, the club began searching for new members: whenever a Tiger was spotted on the road, its owner was traced and sent an application form. The association offered the new member a newsletter, a windscreen decal and a membership card which, if shown to certain parts stores in the area, could result in discount being given on items purchased.

Within a year the club boasted a membership of over 50 enthusiasts. Club activities include rallies, autocrosses and social gatherings. Recently the club decided to become affiliated to Tigers East/Alpines East so that its members

Classic car enthusiasts congregate at the National Classic Concours, Weston Park. (Photo: R. May)

could enjoy the benefits to be gained from being associated with a larger organization.

These, then, are just a few of the Tiger clubs and their activities. Perhaps the words of an enthusiastic American owner sum it up: 'Owning and running a Sunbeam Tiger is the second best way I know of spending money.'

As for spares, one of the primary functions of all Sunbeam Tiger clubs is to help its members obtain replacement parts. In Britain, because of the (relatively) small size of the club, financial resources have meant that only recently has it been possible to contemplate having items such as body panels specially made up. Because of high material, tooling and labour costs, manufacturers prefer large unit quantity orders, making a run of, say, ten wing panels extremely expensive. In America, however, where club memberships are much bigger, those parts which are now unavailable through Chrysler dealers are being made to original patterns by other manufacturers. Even rubber mouldings to fit door surrounds and hardtops are now held by some clubs.

Another advantage of being a member of a club is that from the technical tips published in the club magazines or through casual conversation with other members, one can gain information about interchangeable parts from more modern vehicles, which are, of course, far easier to obtain.

The takeover of Chrysler UK Ltd by the Citroen/Peugeot Company will hardly affect the stocks of Alpine/Tiger spares. It was Chrysler policy to maintain spares for all their vehicles for ten years after production ceased. Beyond that time, stocks have been allowed to lapse. This is quite usual among large manufacturers, being dictated mainly by the limitations of the storage space at their disposal.

Reprints of handbooks, workshop manuals, and even road tests, are still available for the Sunbeam Tiger, either from bookshops specializing in motoring publications, or in many cases through the archives of the Tiger clubs.

British Spares Stockists

American Autoparts, 77 Manor Rd, Wallington, Surrey. Tel. 01-647 4471.

Broadway Speed Centre Ltd., 47 Stoke Newington Church St., London N16. Tel. 01-249 6021.

D.B. Motors of Leicester, 540-542 Aylestone Rd, Leicester LE2 8JB. Tel. 0533 834343/832534.

R. J. Grimes Ltd., Marlpit Lane, Coulsdon, Surrey. Tel. 01-668 1455/6/7.

Wolfrace: Head Office and Mail Order Warehouse, Elms Industrial Estate, Shuttleworth Rd, Goldington, Bedford. Tel. 0234 54232. London Shop Retail, 3 Staples Corner, Edgware Road, London NW2. Tel. 01-450 6231.

US Spares Stockists

Allied Foreign Auto Parts, 601 West Jericho Turnpike, Huntington, NY. Tel. 516 421 0048.

Ansen Wheels, 709 E Walnut St., Carson, Calif. 90746. Tel. 213 327 3080. *Alloy wheels.*

Bap-Geon, 1906 South Main St, Santa Ana, Calif. 92706. Tel. 714 549 3358.

Classics Unlimited, 6 Gerald Ave, Hicksville, NY 11801. *Carpeting and upholstery kits.*

Globe Foreign Parts, 1567 Central Park Ave, Yonkers, NY 10710. Tel. 914 779 8800.

Joppi Foreign Automotive Inc, 5-49 48th Ave, Long Island City, NY 11101.

Long's British Parts Ltd, PO Box 19832, Kansas City, Miss. 64141.

Ormaga Rebuilders, 105 Verdi St, Farmingdale, NY 11735. Tel. 516 752 1216.

Paeco, 213 S 21st St, Birmingham, Ala. 35233.

Ray's Auto Sales, 38 West Broadway, Newport, Rhode Island.

Traction Master Co, 2917 West Olympic Blvd, Los Angeles, Calif. 90006. Tel. 213 382 1131.

World Wide Auto Parts, 208 North York Rd, Bensenville, Ill. 60106. Tel. 312 595 1600.

Clubs

Britain:

Sunbeam Tiger Owners Club: Bill Lynch, pres, 15 Ainslie Rd, Preston, Lancs.

Sunbeam Alpine Owners Club: Chris McGovern, pres, 17 East Field Court, East Acton Lane, London W3 7LB.

Canada:

Canadian Assoc. of Tigers: Peter McDonald, pres, 3814 Oxford St, N. Burnaby, BC U5C 103.

Canadian Assoc. of Tiger Owners: Don Perez, pres, 12428 W. 70th Place, Arvada, Colorado 80004.

Ontario Tiger Owners Assoc: Wolfgang Kaufman, pres, 4000 Tonge St, Apt 223, Toronto, Ontario.

USA:

Sunbeam Tiger Owners Assoc: Paul Voloshin, pres, 14951 San Pablo Ave, San Jose, Calif 95127.

Midwest Tiger Owners Assoc: Don Webb, pres, 2736 Emogene, Melvindale, Mich. 48122.

Sunbeam Tiger Owners, Pacific: Terry Chun, pres, 98-1837 Nahele St, Aiea, Hawaii 96701.

Tigers East/Alpine East: Ron Rogers, pres, PO Box 146, Jessup, Pa. 18434.

California Assoc. of Tigers: Lloyd Law, pres, 5537 Cajon Ave, Buena Park, Calif 90621.

Sunbeam Car Club: Curt Meinel Jr, pres, 202 N. Maples St, Mount Prospect, Ill 60056.

Sunbeam Alpine Club: Stony Barnes, 607 Excalibur Ave, San Jose, Calif 95116.

Pacific Tiger Club: Dennis Grote, pres, 2427 137th S.E. Bellevue, Wash 98006.

Shelby American Automobile Club: 24C April Lane, Norwalk, CT 06850.

Hollywood Sports Cars: 5766 Hollywood Blvd, Hollywood, Calif 90028.

Appendices

	Page

Performance Figures for Sunbeam Alpine Mks I-V

		Series I	Series II	Harrington Le Mans	Series III GT	Series IV GT (auto)	Series V
Autocar road test date		4.5.59	2.12.60	16.2.62	20.9.63	22.5.64	13.5.66
UK price on introduction		£972	£1015	£1494	£889	£853	£875
Average fuel consumption (mpg)		25.5	20.6	20.1	24.9	20.9	25.5
Speeds in the gears	o/d 4	101	98	105	95	92 high	100
	4	91	94	92	98	64 int	96
	o/d 3	82	87	81	95	42 low	94
	3	66	68	65	79		73
	2	45	44	42	51		47
	1	28	28	28	33		30
Acceleration (secs)	0-30	5.1	4.5	4.5	4.5	7.0	4.4
	40	7.1	6.6	6.5	7.0	9.7	6.8
	50	10.6	10.3	9.0	10.1	13.3	9.8
	60	14.0	14.8	13.0	14.9	18.8	13.6
	70	18.4	20.3	17.6	20.8	25.6	18.3
	80	27.5	29.8	24.8	33.0	39.7	26.2
Engine specification	cr	9:1	9:1	9.5:1	9.1:1	9.1:1	9.2:1
	bhp	78 @ 5300	80 @ 5000	96 @ 6000	77 @ 5000	82 @ 5000	92 @ 5500
	torque	89.5 @ 3400	94 @ 3800	105 @ 4500	91 @ 3500	93 @ 3500	110 @ 3700

Sunbeam Tiger Production and Sales Figures

PRODUCTION			SALES					
Date	Chassis nos.		Domestic	Canada	USA	Europe	Other	Total
27. 6.64-31.11.64	B9470001-B9471649	1649 units (Mk I)	18	131	1462	17	21	1649
1. 1.65- 6. 8.65	B9471650-B9473762	2113 units (Mk I)	637	266	1768	206	143	3020
9. 8.65-31.12.65	B382000001-B382000908	908 units (Mk Ia)						
1. 1.66- 9.12.66	B382000909-B382002706	1797 units (Mk Ia)	130	109	1486	78	23	1826
23.12.66-31.12.66	B382100100-B382100129	30 units (Mk II)						
11. 1.67-27. 6.67	B382100130-B382100633	503 units (Mk II)	27	64	292	29	9	421
1968			—	2	101	26	22	151
Total			812	572	5109	356	218	7067

(Sales figures are by courtesy of the California Association of Tiger Owners)

Comparative Production Figures

	1965	1966	1967
Sunbeam Tiger Mk I	3273	1531	
Mk II		32	501
Austin Healey 3000	3944	5494	3051
Sunbeam Alpine	1487	11635	4926
Triumph TR4 and TR4A	13985	11206	6102
MGB (inc. GT)	24703	32916	26524
Jaguar E-type	5370	7059	4989

(Figures by courtesy of the Society of Motor Manufacturers and Traders: figures not available for 1964)

Performance Figures for First Prototype Alpine V8 (tested at MIRA Proving Ground)

Weather conditions
Atmos: 34°F
Boro: 29.1
Wind: 0-5mph south
Specification
Engine: Ford V8 260; AC air cleaner
Transmission: Warner gearbox
Overall ratio: 1st, 7.245:1; 2nd, 5.995:1; 3rd, 4.328:1; top, 3.07:1
Gearbox ratio: 1st, 2.36:1; 2nd, 1.79:1; 3rd, 1.41:1; top, 1:1
Axle: 3.07:1
Tyres: Dunlop 5.90 x 13 RS 5; 24 psi
Test weight: 2984 lb
Average speed consumption
45 mpg: 23.3 mpg

Top Gear	
10-30 mph	5.85 secs
20-40 mph	5.52 secs
20-40 mph	5.52 secs
30-50 mph	5.47 secs
40-60 mph	5.37 secs
50-70 mph	5.82 secs
60-80 mph	7.07 secs
70-90 mph	8.38 secs

3rd Gear	
10-30 mph	3.90 secs
20-40 mph	3.85 secs
30-50 mph	3.95 secs
40-60 mph	4.13 secs
50-70 mph	4.90 secs
60-80 mph	6.64 secs

Thro' Gears	
0-30 mph	3.20 secs
0-40 mph	4.65 secs
0-50 mph	6.75 secs
0-60 mph	8.65 secs
0-70 mph	11.95 secs
0-80 mph	16.00 secs
0-90 mph	20.90 secs

Steady Speed Fuel Consumption:	
30 mph	30.6 mpg
40 mph	32.3 mpg
50 mph	28.6 mpg
60 mph	25.9 mpg
70 mph	23.1 mpg
80 mph	21.0 mpg
90 mph	18.6 mpg

Alpine V8 Performance Figures: comparison between 289 Automatic, 260 Automatic and 289 Manual

Vehicle No	AF 202 '289'	AF 14 '260'	AF 4 '289'
Vehicle weight	3020 lb	3010 lb	3017 lb
Axle ratio	2.88:1	2.88:1	2.88:1
Tyre size	5.90 x 14″	5.90 x 13″	5.90 x 14″

Tyre pressure	26 lb/sq in	26 lb/sq in	26 lb/sq in
Comp ratio	8.8:1	8.8:1	8.8:1
Engine comp pressures (lb/sq in)	140/130/134/150 138/140/135/143	181/194/189/192 163/175/182/185	
Ignition setting	8° btdc @ 510	6° btdc @ 510	
Transmission	Ford automatic	Ford automatic	Ford HEH/B
Weather atmos	55°F	66°F	67°F
Barometer	29.6″ Hg	29.85″ Hg	29.9″ Hg
Wind	0-5 NE	0-12 SE	0-9 SW
Full throttle change points			
1st-2nd	38 mph @ 3900	40 mph @ 4000	47 mph @ 5000
2nd-3rd	68 mph @ 4000	73 mph @ 4200	71 mph @ 5000
3rd-4th			94 mph @ 5000
Thro' gears			
0-30 mph	3.0 secs	3.12 secs	2.75 secs
0-40 mph	4.51 secs	4.58 secs	3.87 secs
0-50 mph	6.46 secs	6.15 secs	5.67 secs
0-60 mph	8.53 secs	7.85 secs	7.28 secs
0-70 mph	11.21 secs	10.38 secs	9.48 secs
0-80 mph	14.91 secs	13.77 secs	12.32 secs
0-90 mph	19.75 secs	18.07 secs	15.77 secs
0-100 mph			21.18 secs
Max speed			
Best lap	116 mph	113.8 mph	
Best ¼ mile	118.2 mph	115.2 mph	
Mean ¼ mile	116.8 mph	113.8 mph	
Fuel consumption steady speed			
30 mph	28.8 mpg	31.3 mpg	32.2 mpg
40 mph	27.4 mpg	30.7 mpg	34.6 mpg
50 mph	25.5 mpg	28.5 mpg	34.0 mpg
60 mph	23.5 mpg	26.8 mpg	30.6 mpg
70 mph	21.2 mpg	23.7 mpg	26.8 mpg
80 mph	19.2 mpg	21.2 mpg	24.2 mpg
90 mph	17.0 mpg	18.3 mpg	20.2 mpg
100 mph	14.9 mpg		
Average speed			
40 mph		24.9 mpg	
45 mph	22.9 mpg	23.5 mpg	

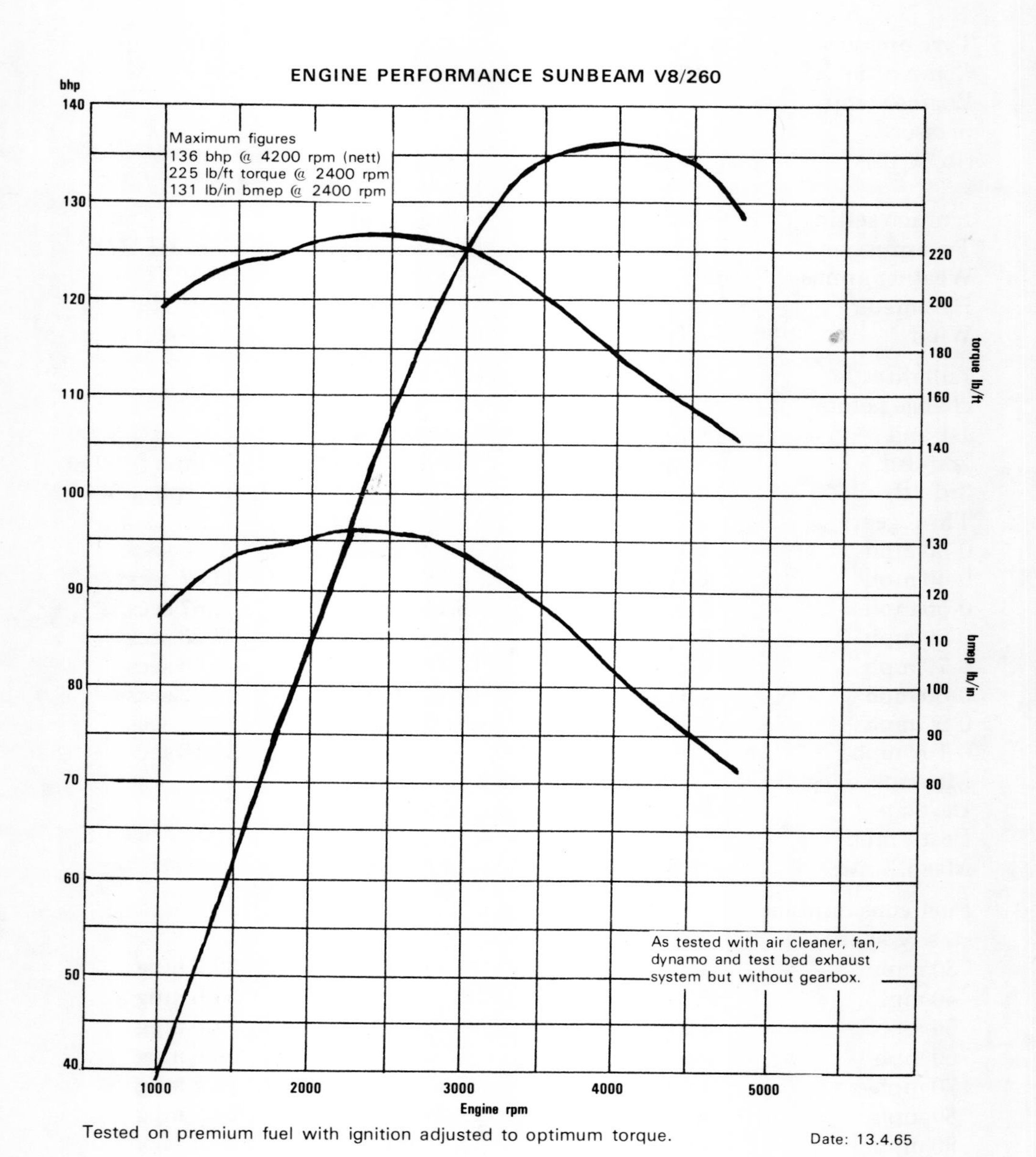

Graph plotting engine performance of Sunbeam Tiger '260'.

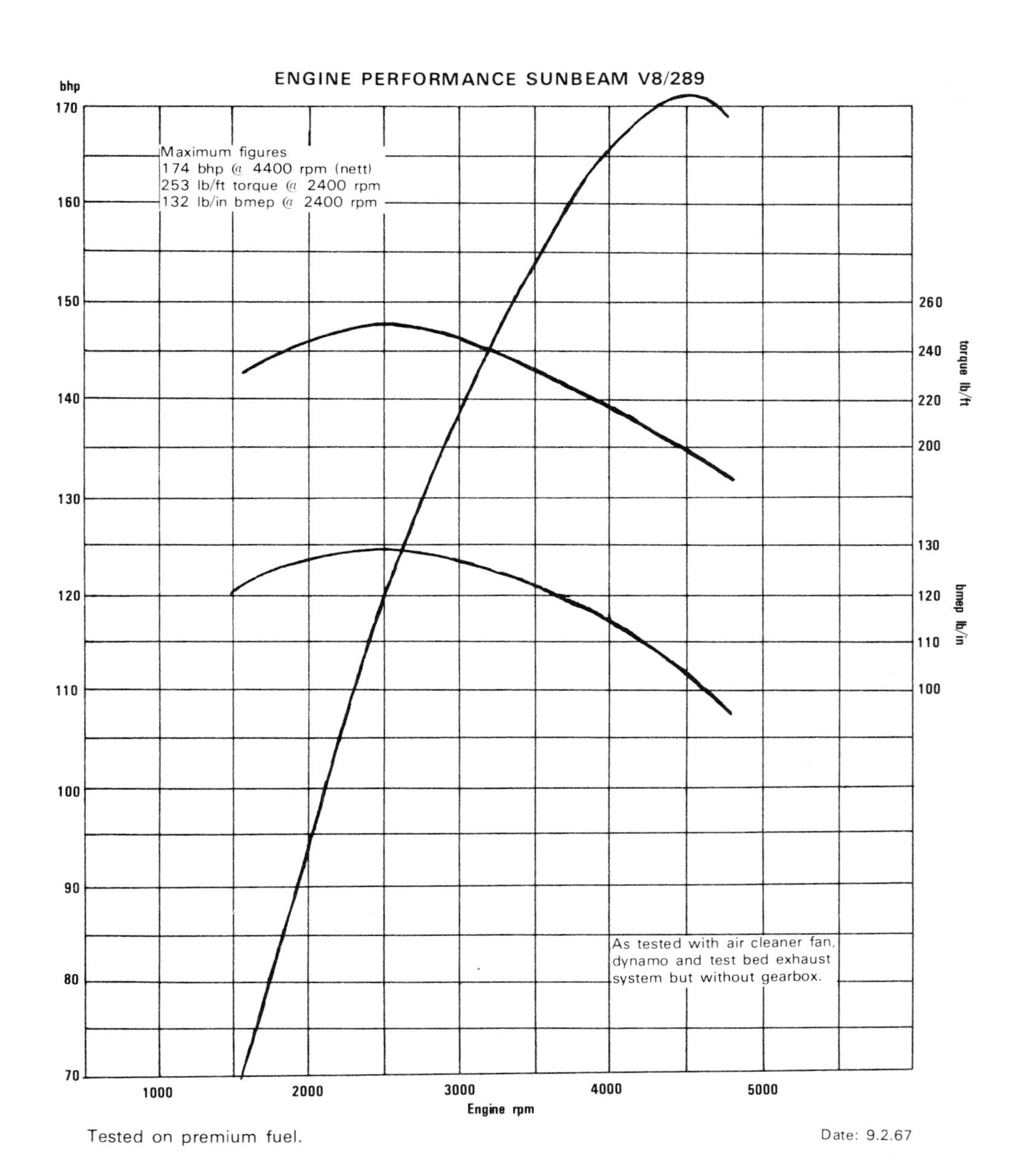

Graph plotting engine performance of Sunbeam Tiger '289'.

Comparative Performance Figures

	Triumph TR4	MGB Tourer	Jaguar E Type 3.8	Sunbeam Alpine III GT	Chevrolet 'Sting Ray'	Austin Healey 3000 Mk III
UK list price on introduction	£1095	£847	£1913	£900	£3432	£1106
Average fuel consumption (mpg)		22	18.6	24.9	14.6	20.3
Speeds in the gears (mph) 4	104	99 (o/d 106)	155	98 (o/d 95)	148	111 (o/d 122)
3	77	83 (o/d 98)	111	79 (o/d 95)	110	83 (o/d 104)
2	51	52	75	51	86	52
1	33	30	42	33	64	43
Acceleration (secs)						
0-30	3.7	4.0	2.5	4.5	3.0	3.4
0-40	5.8	6.0	3.6	7.0	4.1	4.8
0-50	8.3	9.0	5.5	10.0	5.1	7.0
0-60	10.9	12.9	7.2	14.9	6.5	9.5
0-70	14.7	17.2	9.0	20.8	7.3	12.8
0-80	20.9	24.1	12.1	33	10.2	16.2
Engine specification						
cr	9.0:1	8.8:1	9:1	9.1:1	11.25:1	9.0:1
bhp	100 @ 4600	95 @ 5400	265 @ 5500	77 @ 5000	360 @ 6000	148 @ 5250
torque	127 @ 3350	100 @ 3000	260 @ 4000	91 @ 3500	352 @ 4000	165 @ 3500
cc	2138	1798	3781	1592	5363	2912
Autocar road test date	5.1.62	12.2.65	24.4.63	20.9.63	28.2.64	12.6.64

	Mini Cooper S	Aston Martin DB5	Ford Cortina GT	Sunbeam Tiger 260	AC Cobra 4.7	Sunbeam Tiger II
UK list price on introduction	£756	£4248	£780	£1446	£2732	—
Average fuel consumption (mpg)	28	14.7	27	16.9	15.1	19
Speeds in the gears (mph) 4	97	117 (5:142)	94	118	140	122
3	74	95	73	98	116	95
2	54	66	43	74	84	64
1	33	43	29	54	64	44
Acceleration (secs)						
0-30	3.5	3.4	3.7	3.2	2.2	3.1
0-40	6.0	4.4	6.2	5.0	3.2	4.1
0-50	8.2	6.1	9.5	6.8	4.2	5.6
0-60	11.2	8.1	13.9	9.5	5.5	7.5
0-70	15.4	10.8	19.2	12.4	7.3	10.0
0-80	23.4	16.0	31.1	17.5	8.9	13.1
Engine specification						
cr	9.75:1	8.9:1	9.0:1	8.8:1	11:1	9.3:1
bhp	76 @ 5900	28 @ 5500	78 @ 5200	164 @ 4400	300 @ 5750	200 @ 4400
torque	79 @ 3000	280 @ 4500	91 @ 3600	258 @ 2200	285 @ 4500	282 @ 2400
cc	1275	3995	1499	4261	4727	4737
Autocar road test date	14.8.64	18.9.64	8.1.65	30.4.65	12.11.65	Sept 1967 *(Road & Track)*

Performance Figures for Rally Cars (tested at MIRA Proving Ground)

Car 1: Ex-Monte Carlo Rally Tiger — ADU 312B
Tested 11.2.65.
3.77:1 Powr Lok axle ratio. 15 gallons petrol. Full rally specification — spare wheel, jack, etc.
Wind speed 0-8 mph. Ambient 43°F. Track dry.

Car 2: Ex-Alpine Recce Tiger — AHP 295B
Tested 11.8.65.
Shelby cylinder heads. Polished ports. 11:1 compression ratio. Holley carburettors. Chokes 172/173. Jets .067 inch, .078 inch. Inlet valve 1.650. Exhaust valve 1.450. Standard gearbox. 3.77: 1 Powr Lok. 26 gallon tank. Full tank carried. Full rally specification.
Wind speed 0-8 mph. Ambient 70°F. Track dry.
Weight: 1 ton 5 cwt.

Car 3: Sunbeam V8 260 — tested by experimental department
Tested 27.3.65.
Ohv engine. 4280cc. 8.8:1 compression ratio. Ford dual carburettors. Compression pressures: 1-162, 2-164, 3-170, 4-164, 5-164, 6-168, 7-168, 8-171. Gear ratios: 1st-6.81, 2nd-5.76, 3rd-4.06, 4th-2.88. Ignition setting 6° btdc. Carburettor pumps set to maximum. Soft top. Dunlop RS 5 tyres.
Wind speed 0-5 mph. Ambient 46°F. Track dry.
Weight: 2,984 lb (2 up).

Car 4: Team Tiger — AHP 295B
Tested 17.8.65.
Standard 260 cylinder heads. Polished ports. Standard compression ratio. Holley 4 barrel carburettors. Chokes 172/173. Jets .067 inch, .078 inch. Inlet valve 1.665. Exhaust valve 1.450. Shelby high performance camshaft. 26 gallon tank. 25 gallons petrol. Full rally specification. Axle ratio: 3.77:1 Powr Lok.
Wind speed 0-10 mph. Ambient 71°F. Track dry.
Weight: 1 ton 5 cwt.

Car 5: Team Tiger — AHP 295B
Tested 19.8.65.
Standard 260 cylinder heads. Polished ports. Standard compression ratio. 289 2 barrel carburettor. 289 cast iron 2 barrel manifold. Inlet valve 1.665. Exhaust valve 1.450. Shelby high performance camshaft. 26 gallon tank. 25 gallons petrol. Standard gearbox. Full rally specification.

Wind speed 5-12 mph. Ambient 70°F. Track dry.
Weight: 1 ton 5 cwt.

Car 6: Ex-Alpine Rally Austin Healey 3000
Tested 17.8.65.
Tested at MIRA directly after the Alpine Rally, under normal MIRA conditions, ie driver and observer. (See *Autocar* of 3.9.65 for further details of car).

Top Gear	Car 1	Car 2	Car 3	Car 4	Car 5	Car 6
30-40	2.2	2.4	2.85	2.3	2.65	
40-50	2.2	2.3	3.15	2.25	2.45	
50-60	2.3	2.35	2.80	2.3	2.55	
60-70	2.5	2.45	3.43	2.4	2.9	
70-80	2.18	2.8	4.15	3.8	3.3	
80-90	3.1	3.2	5.22	3.8	3.9	
90-100	4.0	4.5	—	—	—	
3rd Gear						
30-40	—	1.8	2.0	1.7	1.9	
40-50	1.8	1.7	2.3	1.65	1.85	
50-60	2.0	1.8	2.2	1.75	2.05	
60-70	2.4	2.1	2.9	2.15	2.35	
70-80	—	2.5	3.9	2.7	3.1	
Thro' Gears						
0-30	—	3.0	3.55	2.75	2.8	2.7
0-40	—	4.9	3.5	3.55	3.95	4.7
0-50	5.5	4.9	7.0	4.7	5.4	6.1
0-60	7.5	6.8	9.2	6.45	8.0	8.2
0-70	9.8	9.35	12.25	9.25	10.85	10.2
0-80	12.4	11.4	16.27	11.5	14.1	12.9
0-90	—	14.6	—	14.9	18.6	16.0
0-100	—	19.5	—	19.0	—	19.2
						(0-110 23.5)

		Car 1	Car 2	Car 3	Car 4	Car 5	Car 6
Standing ¼ mile	(secs)	15.4	14.8	21.7	14.7	15.9	15.6
	(mph)		92		89	84	
Best flying ¼ mile	(secs)	7.9	8.0		7.8	7.9	Max speed in
	(mph)	113.0	112.5		115.3	113.9	OD top: 120
Mean flying ¼ mile	(secs)	7.8	8.1		7.8	8.0	top: 100
	(mph)	115.0	112.1		114.6	112.5	
Lap speed	(secs)	92.0	94.0		92.7	93.7	
	(mph)	110.0	108		109	108	

Performance Figures for Alpine V8 compared with Austin Healey 3000 Mk II and Mk III

	V8	Healey Mk III		Healey Mk II	
Thro' gears	(secs)	(secs)		(secs)	
0-30 mph	3.55	3.6		3.2	
0-40 mph	5.00	4.8		5.1	
0-50 mph	7.00	6.9		7.2	
0-60 mph	9.20	9.8		10.3	
0-70 mph	12.25	12.1		12.9	
0-80 mph	16.25	14.8		16.7	
0-90 mph	21.7	18.2		21.3	
0-100 mph		23.7		29.4	
0-110 mph		34.1		45.3	
Top Gear		Direct	Overdrive	Direct	Overdrive
10-30 mph	6.23			7.5	9.6
20-40 mph	5.92	6.0	9.0	7.2	9.6
30-50 mph	6.00	6.8	10.5	7.2	9.9
40-60 mph	5.95	6.8	9.0	7.4	10.0
50-70 mph	6.23	6.7	9.4	7.8	11.1
60-80 mph	7.58	7.9	11.0	8.2	11.2
70-90 mph	9.37	7.6	11.2	9.1	12.1
80-100 mph		8.6	13.2		14.9
90-110 mph			16.7		24.8
Next to top					
10-30 mph	4.40	4.3		5.5	
20-40 mph	4.10	5.1		5.2	
30-50 mph	4.30	5.2		5.1	
40-60 mph	4.50	4.9		5.1	
50-70 mph	5.10	5.7		5.9	
60-80 mph	6.80				
Maximum speed	125	122.5	116 (5,500 rpm)	112.5	106 (5,600 rpm)
Fuel Consumption					
30 mph	33.8 mpg	28.2 mpg	32.6 mpg	29¼ mpg	37 mpg
40 mph	33.1 mpg	28.2 mpg	31.8 mpg	28 mpg	31¼ mpg
50 mph	29.6 mpg	27.2 mpg	30.5 mpg	25¼ mpg	28¼ mpg
60 mph	27.2 mpg	26.0 mpg	29.0 mpg	23 mpg	26 mpg
70 mph	24.0 mpg	23.8 mpg	28.0 mpg	22 mpg	24¾ mpg
80 mph	21.7 mpg	22.0 mpg	24.9 mpg	20½ mpg	21¾ mpg
90 mph	19.6 mpg	19.5 mpg	22.0 mpg	18¾ mpg	20¾ mpg
100 mph		17.4 mpg	19.0 mpg		18½ mpg
Tyre size	5.90 x 13	5.90 x 15		5.90 x 15	
Axle Ratio	2.88	3.545	2.91	3.909	3.205
mph/1000 rpm	24	20.5	25.0	20.5	25.0

Alpine V8/Tiger Prototypes

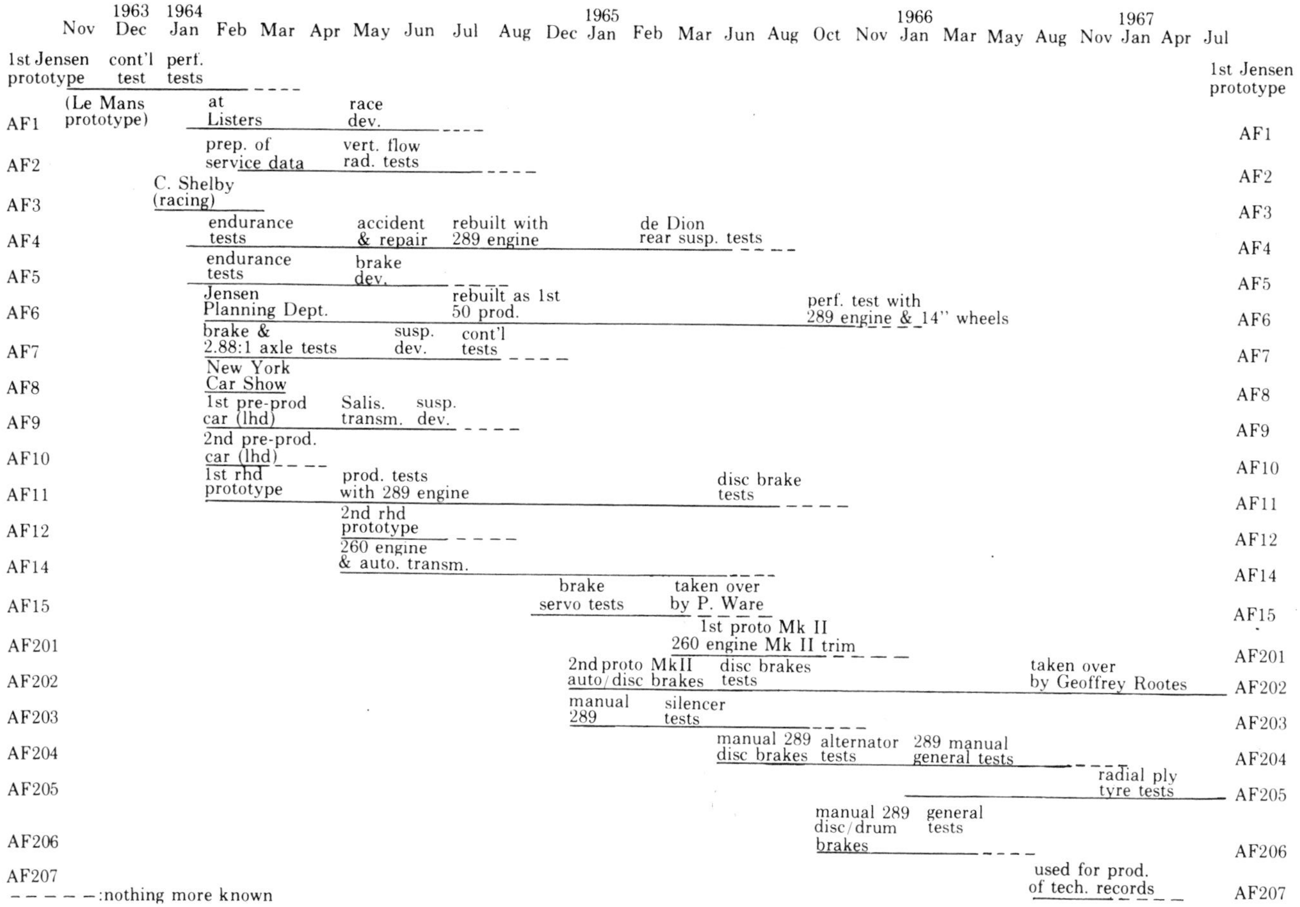

1963 1964 1965 1966 1967
Nov Dec Jan Feb Mar Apr May Jun Jul Aug Dec Jan Feb Mar Jun Aug Oct Nov Jan Mar May Aug Nov Jan Apr Jul

1st Jensen prototype: cont'l test; perf. tests — 1st Jensen prototype

AF1: (Le Mans prototype); at Listers; race dev. — AF1

AF2: prep. of service data; vert. flow rad. tests — AF2

AF3: C. Shelby (racing) — AF3

AF4: endurance tests; accident & repair; rebuilt with 289 engine; de Dion rear susp. tests — AF4

AF5: endurance tests; brake dev. — AF5

AF6: Jensen Planning Dept.; rebuilt as 1st 50 prod.; perf. test with 289 engine & 14" wheels — AF6

AF7: brake & 2.88:1 axle tests; susp. dev.; cont'l tests — AF7

AF8: New York Car Show — AF8

AF9: 1st pre-prod car (lhd); Salis. transm.; susp. dev. — AF9

AF10: 2nd pre-prod. car (lhd) — AF10

AF11: 1st rhd prototype; prod. tests with 289 engine; disc brake tests — AF11

AF12: 2nd rhd prototype — AF12

AF14: 260 engine & auto. transm. — AF14

AF15: brake servo tests; taken over by P. Ware — AF15

AF201: 1st proto Mk II 260 engine Mk II trim — AF201

AF202: 2nd proto MkII auto/disc brakes; disc brakes tests; taken over by Geoffrey Rootes — AF202

AF203: manual 289; silencer tests — AF203

AF204: manual 289 disc brakes; alternator tests; 289 manual general tests — AF204

AF205: radial ply tyre tests — AF205

AF206: manual 289 disc/drum brakes; general tests — AF206

AF207: used for prod. of tech. records — AF207

- - - - - :nothing more known

Summary of Works Tigers' Race and Rally Results, 1964-1966

Event	Date	Car	Driver/co-driver	Result
Races				
Le Mans 24 Hours	June 1964	ADU 179B	C. Dubois/K. Ballisat	retired
		ADU 180B	J Blumer/P. Proctor	retired
Targa Florio	May 1965	AHP 483B	P. Harper/R. Jones	2nd in class
Freddie Dixon Trophy	1966	Fraser Tiger	B. Unett	1st in class 2nd overall
Autosport Championship	1966	Fraser Tiger	B. Unett	1st in class 2nd overall
Rallies				
Geneva	Oct. 1964	ADU 310B	T. Lewis/A. Hedges	1st in class
		ADU 311B	P. Riley/R. Turvey	2nd in class
		ADU 312B	R. Smith/M. Mackenzie	3rd in class
RAC	Nov. 1964	AHP 483B	R. Jones/J. Clegg	crashed
Monte Carlo	Jan. 1965	ADU 312B	P. Harper/I. Hall	1st in class
		AHP 295B	A. Cowan/R. Turvey	2nd in class
Tulip	Apr. 1965	ADU 311B	P. Harper/I. Hall	retired
			P. Riley/R. Turvey	retired
International Police	May 1965	AHP 295B	J. Gott/D. Nicholson	outright winner
Alpine	July 1965	ADU 312B	P. Harper/Hughes	disqualified
		ADU 311B	T. Lewis	crashed
		AHP 295B	I. Hall	retired
RAC	Nov. 1965	ADU 311B	P. Harper/D. Barrow/P. Riley	
Scottish	June 1965	EGA 65C	J. Melvin/H. Wilson	1st in class
			A. Cowan/A. Redpath	retired
Monte Carlo	Jan. 1966	FRW 667C	A. Cowan/I. Hall	crashed
		AHP 295B	P. Harper/R. Turvey	retired
Tulip	April 1966	FRW 668C	P. Harper/R. Turvey	1st in class
Acropolis	May 1966	ADU 311B	P. Harper/I. Hall	1st in class

Summary of Sunbeam Alpine and Tiger Successes in Major Events, 1964-1966

Summary of Sunbeam Alpine and Tiger Successes in Major Events, 1964-1966
1964 International Scottish Rally (18-22 May)
1301-2500 cc Grand Touring cars: 2nd, John Melvin/Hamish Wilson (Sunbeam Alpine); 3rd, Michael Butler/Jack Henley (Sunbeam Alpine).
1964 Pacific Divisional Championships — Willow Springs California (13 June)
1st in class 'B' production event: Lew Spencer (Sunbeam Tiger) at 89 mph.
1964 Sports Car Club of America National Championship
1st in class 'F': Don Sesslar (Sunbeam Alpine).
1964 US 200 Mile National Sports Car Race — Elkhart Lake (12 September)
1st in class and 2nd overall: Lew Spencer (Sunbeam Tiger).
1964 Geneva Rally (15-18 October)
Over 2500 cc GT class: 1st, I. D. Lewis/B. Hughes (Sunbeam Tiger); 2nd P. Riley/R. Turvey (Sunbeam Tiger); 3rd, Miss R. Smith/Miss M. MacKenzie (Sunbeam Tiger).
1964 Panama Grand Prix (7 November)
1st in 1500-2000 cc class and 3rd overall: Michael Reed (Sunbeam Alpine).
1964 International Rally of Great Britain (7-13 November)
Club and Ecurie team prize: J. La Trobe/J. Chitty (Sunbeam Alpine).
1965 Monte Carlo Rally (16-23 January)
Over 2,500 cc GT Class: 1st, P. Harper/I. Hall (Sunbeam Tiger); 2nd, A. Cowan/R. Turvey (Sunbeam Tiger). Overall placings: 4th, P. Harper/I. Hall (Sunbeam Tiger); 11th, A. Cowan/R. Turvey (Sunbeam Tiger).

Awards won by P. Harper (Sunbeam Tiger): Cup of the Commission Sportive of the ISC (for class win); Challenge Antony Noghes (for the highest placed competitor who has taken part in at least 10 Monte Carlo Rallies) — won by Harper for the 3rd time, thus gaining the trophy outright; RAC Challenge Trophy (for the highest placed British driver of a British car).
Dutch National 24 Hour Records (February 1965)
New records established by Rob Slotemaker and David Van Lennop in a Sunbeam Tiger on the Zandvort Circuit, Holland:

3 hours at 76.54 mph (123.163 kph)
6 hours at 76.14 mph (122.526 kph)
12 hours at 75.0 mph (120.69 kph)
24 hours at 75.47 mph (120.163 kph)
Total distance 1,792.07 miles (2883.93 km)

1965 Danville Virginia National Races, USA (10-11 April)
1st in class 'B' and 2nd overall: Don Sesslar (Sunbeam Tiger); 1st in class 'F': Dan Carmichael (Sunbeam Alpine); 2nd in class 'F': Al Coftner (Sunbeam Alpine).

1965 International Police Rally, Belgium (29-30 May)
Outright winner: J. Gott/D. E. Nicholson (Sunbeam Tiger).
Santa Barbara Road Races, USA (29 May)
Class 'B' production cars: 1st, J. Adams (Sunbeam Tiger).
Mosport (Players 200 Meeting), Canada (5 June)
Production sports cars race: 1st, J. Adams (Sunbeam Tiger).
1965 International Scottish Rally (7-11 June)
1st in over 2,500 cc GT class: J. Melvin/H. Wilson (Sunbeam Tiger).
Stockton Road Races, California (12 June)
Class 'B' production cars: 1st, J. Adams (Sunbeam Tiger).
Salt Lake City Utah National Points Races (11 July)
Class win: J. Adams (Sunbeam Tiger).
San Louis Obispo Road Races, California (14 August)
Outright win: J. Adams (Sunbeam Tiger).
Daytona 24 Hour Race (February 1966)
1st Ladies award: Miss R. Smith/Miss "Smokey" Drolet (Sunbeam Alpine).
Caracas Cup Race, Venezuela (March 1966)
1st in class: (Sunbeam Tiger).
International Tulip Rally (April 1966)
1st in the GT category and 1st in the over 2,500 cc class: P. Harper/R. Turvey (Sunbeam Tiger).
Governors Cup Race, Maracay, Venezuela (April 1966)
1st in class (Sunbeam Tiger).
Arboe Night Rally, Austria (April 1966)
1st in class and best performance (Sunbeam Tiger).
Veralpen Rally, Austria (April 1966)
1st overall and 1st in class: Schindler (Sunbeam Tiger).
Acropolis International Rally (May 1966)
1st in class over 2,000 cc GT and 2nd overall in GT category: P. Harper/I. Hall (Sunbeam Tiger).
International Austrian Alpine Rally (May 1966)
1st in over 2,000 cc GT class: Schindler/Naser (Sunbeam Tiger).
International Martha Journalists Rally, Austria (May 1966)
1st in 1600 cc GT class: A. Stachl (Sunbeam Alpine).
Gran Premio de Tenerife (May 1966)
1st overall: R. Spencer (Sunbeam Tiger).
Las Palmas Circuit Race (May 1966)
1st overall: R. Spencer (Sunbeam Tiger).
Austrian Championship Hill Climb (June 1966)
1st overall: C. Schindler (Sunbeam Tiger).
Kottingsbrunn Slalom, Austria (June 1966)
1st overall: C. Schindler (Sunbeam Tiger).

Finnish Sports Car Championship Race (June 1966)
1st in class: Miss T. Ketchen (Sunbeam Tiger).
Grenzland Rally, Austria (September 1966)
1st in overall GT category and 1st in class (GT over 1600 cc): C. Schindler (Sunbeam Tiger).
Los Angeles Times GP Class 'B' Production Race, Riverside, California (October 1966)
1st: R. Dykes (Sunbeam Tiger).
Freddie Dixon Trophy (1966)
1st in class and 2nd overall: B. Unett (Sunbeam Tiger).
Autosport Championship
1st in class and 2nd overall: B. Unett (Sunbeam Tiger).

Competition Options for Sunbeam Tiger Mk I as available from Rootes' Competitions Department, Coventry, 1965-1966

The engine can be tuned in the following stages:

		£ s. d.
	STAGE 1	
1.	High Performance Cam Kit. Lift is .300″, timing duration 306°. This increases the stock 141 hp rating to approximately 161 hp. Kit includes: 1 camshaft and 16 solid tappets.	25.15.0
2.	High Performance Distributor Kit. A twin point heavy duty distributor, with a competition curve, delivering a reliable spark at high rpm. Used with colder BF.603 sparking plugs, there will be a gain of five horse power. Kit includes: 1 distributor and 8 BF.601 sparking plugs.	18.10.2
3.	Heavy Duty Valve Springs — 16. Advisable for speeds of over 5000 rpm. It is recommended that items 1, 2 and 3 be fitted as a single stage.	9.18.8
	STAGE II, WITH ITEMS 1 TO 3	
4.	With the valve lift and duration allowing better breathing, it is now possible to increase the induction capacity by fitting the Four Barrel Induction Kit, giving a further 55 hp. Kit includes: 1 intake manifold. 1 four barrel carburettor.	68. 4.4

5. To ensure adequate petrol supply at the carburettor, a High Pressure Twin Barrel Pump is fitted, with large bore piping.
Kit includes: 1 high pressure petrol pump. 2 pump fixing brackets. Length of petrol pipe. 13. 6.6

STAGE III, WITH ITEMS 1 TO 5.

6. Polished Cylinder Heads, with flowed ports, gives further increase in horse power. 31.10.0

7. Heavy Duty Clutch Kit, for increased efficiency at high rpm.
Kit includes: 1 pressure plate assembly. 1 clutch disc. 28.11.0

Additional modifications to the engine, in the interest of reliability are:

8. A competition sump, with anti-surge swing baffles, fitted giving increased capacity. 47. 5.0

9. Strengthened Oil Pump Pick-up Pipe. 1.10.0

10. Fitting Threaded Valve Rocker Posts into cylinder heads, strongly recommended for high engine speeds. 25. 6.4

11. Removing pressed in oil gallery plugs and fitting threaded type (price when engine is stripped). 3.15.0

12. Fitting a flexible pipe to the clutch slave cylinder. 3.15.0

13. *Complete Engine Gasket set. 8.10.11
*Top Overhaul Gasket set. 6. 5.9

14. *Competition Exhaust System, giving an increase in power and more ground clearance, essential for competition work. 30. 0.0
NOTE: The fitting of this item necessitates the modifying of the cross member holes and re-locating the petrol pump.

15. Engine Sump Guard. 17.10.0

16. High Efficiency Radiator, of increased capacity. 50. 0.0
An Engine Oil Cooler Kit. 35. 0.0

Both items are essential for competition use.
NOTE: The fitting of the above items requires extensive modification to the engine compartment front apron, and forward bulkhead.

17.	*Revolution Counter, calibrated to 8000 rpm	9.15.0
18.	26 Gallon Petrol Tank Kit.	37. 0.0
	Unit and Gauge.	3.10.0
	Tank Retaining Straps.	
	2 Sheets of Sorbo rubber.	1.10.0
	5 Ply Board.	1.10.0
	NOTE: The fitting of this item requires extensive modification to the boot.	
	CHASSIS	
19.	*Brakes. It is necessary to fit competition brake linings and pads, and change to competition fluid.	
	1 set of rear brake shoes and linings.	4. 1.6
	1 set of front brake pads.	4. 0.0
	1 qt. of brake fluid.	18.0
20.	*Front Suspension, Competition Springs and Shock Absorbers.	
	2 front springs @ £3.0.0.	£6. 0.0
	2 front shock absorbers @ £4.0.0.	£8. 0.0
21.	*Rear Suspension, Competition Springs and Shock Absorbers.	
	2 rear springs @ £7.10.0.	15. 0.0
	2 rear shock absorbers @ £4.10.0	9. 0.0
22.	Rear Axle.	
	The following ratios are available and can be supplied with or without a limited slip differential (standard axle 2.88 to 1).	
	3.31 3.54 3.77	
	Exchange price for alternative ratios.	24. 0.0
	Exchange price for Powr Lok — all ratios.	35. 0.0
	A rebate will be given depending on the condition of the exchange axle.	
23.	*Speedometer for all ratios.	4.17.6
24.	Lightweight magnesium wheels, essential for competition use.	
	5 lightweight magnesium wheels.	71. 0.0
	1 pack (18) chrome special wheel nuts.	6. 0.0
	2 spacers for front wheels.	15.0

5 Dunlop SP.41 tyres @£8.19.0.	44.15.0
5 tubes @ 19.0.	4.15.0
Modification to the front and rear wheel arches, to offer extra tyre clearance.	3.10.0

It cannot be too strongly emphasized that the standard steel wheels are only suitable for road use, and it will be necessary to fit magnesium alloy wheels if the car is to be used for any form of competition. There will be an added charge for balance.

*Items so marked — dealer normal discount applies. All other parts are nett.

Factory Options for Sunbeam Tiger Mk I as available through Rootes Motors Inc., USA, 1965-1966

Part No.	Description	List Price
LAT-1*	Super induction kit — (Hi-Rise manifold and Holley 4-bbl. carb.)	$140.00
LAT-2	Dress-up kit — polished aluminium rocker covers, chrome air cleaner, radiator and oil filler cap.	$69.00
LAT-4	Large capacity aluminium oil pan.	$86.00
LAT-5	Traction-Master anti-tramp rods.	$42.25
LAT-7	Steel N.H.R.A. & A.H.R.A. approved scatter shield	$100.00
LAT-8	Polished aluminium rocker arm covers.	$40.00
LAT-10	Tiger key chain.	$1.50
LAT-12	Tiger ash tray (for den or office).	$ .85
LAT-13	Tiger pocket lighter	$1.50
LAT-14	Tiger embroidered jacket patch.	$2.00
LAT-15	Tiger flag set.	$3.00
LAT-16	Tiger decals	$ .15
LAT-17	Men's Tiger "tee-shirts"	$1.70
LAT-18	Tiger rally jacket	$8.50
LAT-20*	Hi-lift camshaft kit — complete with $\frac{3}{4}$ solid lifter camshaft, 16 solid lifters, 16 outer, 16 inner valve springs, gaskets, one dual-point distributor.	$100.00

*The LAT-1 & LAT-20 kits are used on the 245 BHP engine.
The LAT-1 kit when supplied separately is fitted with a Holley No. 1-12-4-bbl. carburettor of 465 c.f.m. for use with the hydraulic lifter camshaft.

When the LAT-1 and LAT-20 kits are ordered as original equipment on the 245 BHP Tiger, the carburettor is a Holley R-3259-AS, 4-bbl. of 715 c.f.m.

Part No.	Description	List Price
LAT-21	Lightweight horns.	$15.00
LAT-22	7,000 R.P.M. tachometer	$55.00
LAT-25	Fibreglass hood air-scoop for fitting on standard hood.	$15.00
LAT-27	Cast-iron low restriction exahust manifolds	$65.00
LAT-48	Jacket pocket patch Tiger.	$ .75
LAT-50	Limited-slip differential (must use LAT-51, 52, 53, 54 ring gear and pinion set).	$110.00
LAT-51	Crown wheel and pinion 3.07:1 ratio.	$50.00
LAT-52	3.31:1 ratio set.	$50.00
LAT-53	3.54:1 ratio set.	$50.00
LAT-54	3.73:1 ratio set.	$50.00
LAT-58	Chrome silver Tiger tail stripe kit.	$3.50
LAT-60	Heavy-duty street clutch set, pressure plate and disc.	$50.50
LAT-63	Boy's "tee-shirt"	$1.50
LAT-67	Men's heavy sweat shirt.	$3.00
LAT-70	Polished aluminium 5.50x13 wheels, each:	$48.00
LAT-73	Competition header kit.	$140.00
LAT-74	Low restriction exhaust muffler kit.	$52.00
LAT-76	Hi-speed HD shock absorber — rear	$16.85
LAT-77	Hi-speed HD front shocks.	$16.85
LAT-79	Lightweight fibreglass hood, with air-scoop and engine heat exhaust outlets.	$135.00
LAT-80	Lightweight, fibreglass 6 blade engine fan, variable-pitch at high rpm for minimum drag.	

Index